Mystics *after* Modernism

CLASSICS IN ANTHROPOSOPHY

Anthroposophy (A Fragment)

Autobiography

Christianity as Mystical Fact

How to Know Higher Worlds

Intuitive Thinking as a Spiritual Path

Nature's Open Secret

An Outline of Esoteric Science

The Souls' Awakening—A Mystery Drama

The Spiritual Guidance of the Individual and Humanity

Theosophy

A Way of Self-Knowledge

Mystics *after* Modernism

DISCOVERING THE SEEDS OF A NEW SCIENCE IN THE RENAISSANCE

Rudolf Steiner

Translated by Karl E. Zimmer

& Anthroposophic Press

dedicated to Paul Allen

This book is a translation of *Die Mystik im Augange des neuzeitlichen Geisteslebens und ihr Verhältnis zur modernen Weltanschauung*, GA7, published by Rudolf Steiner Nachlassverwaltung, Dornach, Switzerland.

Published by Anthroposophic Press

This edition copyright 2000 by Anthroposophic Press

Library of Congress Cataloging-in-Publication Data

Steiner, Rudolf, 1861-1925.
[Mystik im Aufgange des neuzeitlichen Geisteslebens und ihr Verhältnis zur modernen Weltanschauung. English]
Mystics after modernism ; discovering the seeds of a new science in the Renaissance / Rudolf Steiner ; translated by Karl E. Zimmer.
p. cm.—(Classics in anthroposophy)
Includes bibliographical references and index.
ISBN: 0-88010-470-8 (pbk.)
1. Mysticism—History. I. Title. II. Series

BV5075.S813 2000
299'.935–dc21   00-030615

All rights in this book are reserved. No part of this book may be reproduced in any form without written permission from the publishers except for brief quotations embodied in critical articles for reviews.

Contents

Foreword by Christopher Bamford *7*
Preface to the 1923 Edition *13*
Introduction: Mystics, Natural Science,
  and the Modern World *17*
Meister Eckhart *37*
The Friendship with God *49*
Cardinal Nicholas of Cusa *71*
Agrippa of Nettesheim & Theophrastus Paracelsus *89*
Valentin Weigel & Jacob Boehme *105*
Giordano Bruno & Angelus Silesius *115*
Epilogue *126*
Afterword: About the Author, the People and
  the Background of This Book *131*
Preface to the First Edition: 1901 .... *197*
Bibliography and Further Reading *201*
Index *205*

Foreword

by Christopher Bamford

THIS IS A MOST REMARKABLE BOOK. Though one hundred years old (the substance of it was given as lectures in the fall of 1900), it is as relevant and vital as it ever was, perhaps even more so. Steiner's approach might have seemed obscure and peripheral to mainstream thinking when he wrote, but by now history has caught up with him. Much of what he says could have been written today.

Indeed, we may say that when Steiner—a philosopher and sometime journalist, who had written books on Goethe, Nietzsche, and the theory of knowledge—decided to "come out" before an audience of Theosophists with what he truly believed, the sense of urgency (both personal and cultural) to which he was responding allowed him to say something truly prophetic: namely, that if we are to redeem the one-dimensional scientific worldview of modernism, we must do so by picking up where the mystics and humanists of the late Middle Ages and early Renaissance left off, integrating their insights and ways of knowing with what we have gained from modern science to create a new "spiritual science," at once "mystical" and scientific. This thesis, revolutionary for its time, has now been borne out and confirmed by recent research done in the fields of mysticism and the origins of modern science since Steiner wrote.

Stephen Toulmin, for example, in *Cosmopolis: The Hidden Agenda of Modernity,* besides revealing the origins of "rational," theory-centered, scientific modernity in the chaos and uncertainty of the religious wars of the seventeenth century, points to humanists like Montaigne and Rabelais (and even Shakespeare) as "postmodern" before the fact: open-minded; in love with particular, concrete experience; able to see the universal in the local; and able to live with paradox.[1] In other words, Toulmin sees true (post)modernity arising in the early Renaissance and then being superseded, after a violent struggle—Bruno, after all, was burned at the stake—by the scientific modernism of Galileo, Descartes, and Newton.

The war between the diametrically opposed worldview of humanistic "magic" and natural science has been amply documented by the late Dame Frances Yates. In *Giordano Bruno and the Hermetic Tradition*, for instance, she shows how Marin Mersenne, the friend and correspondent of Descartes and Gassendi and the admirer of Galileo, regarded Bruno as the most wicked and most dangerous man who ever lived on earth, simply because *he wished to place the whole world within consciousness.*[2] The assumption of the primacy of consciousness inevitably led to a world that was anathema to the "good father." Mersenne fought it with every fibre of his being. Bruno being no more, Mersenne took as his opponent Robert Fludd, the Rosicrucian. (Rosicrucianism was the last attempt to fulfil the true Renaissance dream, as Rudolf Steiner acknowledged by proclaiming his anthroposophy its continuation.)

As Frances Yates says: "Mersenne is a modern; he has crossed the watershed and is on the same side of it as we are." But not all of us, and not all to the same degree. Throughout the seventeenth century, as feminist historians of science have shown us, a more holistic, consciousness-based, gentler, more "feminine" science—epitomized in the "rosicrucianism" of such figures as Van Helmont—

---

1. Stephen Toulmin, *Cosmopolis: The Hidden Agenda of Modernity.*
2. Frances A Yates, *Giordano Bruno and the Hermetic Tradition.* Other books by Yates include, *The Rosicrucian Enlightenment* and *The Occult Philosophy of the Elizabethan Age.* On Bruno, see Ramon G. Mendoza, *The Acentric Labyrinth: Giordano Bruno's Prelude to Contemporary Cosmology.* See bibliography.

continued to develop.[3] And, besides that, though we have still to fully realize it, we are now and already "post-modern." The world of Descartes, Newton, and Kant no longer works.

This, then, is the field into which Steiner's little book—short in length but deep in content—fits, tracking the spiritual and epistemological struggle for modernism by means of a consideration of eleven European "mystics": Eckhart, Tauler, Suso, Ruysbroeck, Nicholas of Cusa, Agrippa von Nettesheim, Paracelsus, Valentin Weigel, Jacob Boehme, Giordano Bruno and Johann Scheffler (called Angelus Silesius). Again, Steiner is amazingly modern in understanding the continuity of thinking from the Middle Ages (Eckhart) into the early Renaissance (Nicholas of Cusa) and on to the final flowering in Bruno and Silesius. In this way, he shows us a real, *evolving* stream or current of consciousness, which is still available and still evolving. By engaging it today, he claims, we can redeem and transform scientific mechanistic dualism.

There has been much research in the area of mysticism, of course, since Steiner wrote. In fact, the last century has witnessed a veritable revolution in this field. Most important, perhaps, we now recognize the enormous formative foundation provided by women mystics such as Hildegard of Bingen, Beatrice of Nazareth, Gertrud of Helfta, Hadewich, Margaret of Porete, and the two Mechtilds—of Hackeborn and of Magdeburg.[4] But Steiner's thesis

---

3. See Carolyn Marchant, *The Death of Nature: Women, Ecology, and the Scientific Revolution*; see also the work of Evelyn Fox Keller, and on Van Helmont, see Walter Pagel *Joan Baptista Van Helmont: Reformer of Science and Medicine*.

4. The literature is enormous and always growing. See, among others, Bernard McGinn (ed), *Meister Eckhart and the Beguine Mystics: Hadewijch of Brabant, Mechtild of Magdeburg and Marguerite of Porete*; also Oliver Davies, *Meister Eckhart, Mystic Theologian*; Bernard McGinn, *The Flowering of Mysticism: Men and Women in the new Mysticism—1200-1350*; Amy Hollywood, *The Soul as Virgin Wife: Mechtild of Magdeburg, Marguerite of Porete, and Meister Eckhart*; Carolyn Walker Bynum, *Jesus as Mother: Studies in the Spirituality of the High Middle Ages*; Peter Dronke, *Women Writers of the Middle Ages: A Critical Study of texts from Perpetua (d. 203) to Marguerite of Porete (d. 1310)*; Barbara Newman, *Sister of Wisdom: Saint Hildegard's Theology of the Feminine*; see bibliography.

is not affected by his ignorance of the very real influence of these women on the men he writes about. Indeed, knowing about these women and, as it were, mentally adding some chapters at the beginning of his book, only makes his thesis stronger and gives it more bite.

This thesis is, essentially, that mysticism is *a way of knowing*, an experimental, phenomenological attentiveness to various modalities of consciousness or experience. As such, in principle, it is as applicable to "outer" natural experience—science—as it is to "inner" experience. Steiner's introduction, an astonishing tour de force of epistemology, makes this clear. He begins by quoting Hegel's defence against those who would dismiss philosophy as mere abstraction. "No, no," Hegel writes, "They are acts of universal spirit.... The philosophers are closer to the master than those who feed upon the crumbs of the spirit. They read or write the orders from on high in the original; it is their function to take part in writing them. The philosophers are the mystics who were present at the act in the innermost sanctuary and who participated in it." That is to say that human consciousness can participate in the living, creative thoughts that underlie the world. This is not thought as computation or dialectical reasoning. It is thought—living thinking—as real and universal, as Steiner puts it, beyond "the incidental individual personality of the beholder." This is the world to which the deep self-knowledge of the mystics gave them access. Such a world, as Steiner says, requires a new sense corresponding to it. Lacking that sense, we are blind to that world: it does not exist.

Now, for the mystic, that new world and the organ for perceiving it are the same, the soul. The path is one of "self-knowledge." "In all other kinds of knowing the object is outside ourselves; in self-knowledge we stand inside the object." Exterior objects come to us closed and finished; interior objects, in whose coming into being we participate, remain open and inexhaustible. Both "come" to us, but they come to us differently. Thus, there is a similarity and difference. The "objects"—whether "inner" or "outer"—remain independent of us, other, and communicate with us, speak to us in a language. "The same language that reaches from the realm of [outer] objects, we also hear inside ourselves. But then is *we* who are speaking. It is only a matter of listening aright to the transformation that occurs when we close our perception to external things and listen only to what then sounds in ourselves."

What happens when we listen in this way to the language objects speak? *We become what we know.* This is a process of "awakening to the self." But it is not a little self, but a self that is ultimately one with the universe. Thou art that, *Tat tvam asi*, as the Hindus say. Our self expands. With it, our consciousness is raised, our understanding is deepened. This is an infinite (indefinite) process. It is not a change in the content of consciousness, but in its structure. As Steiner writes, "What I add to things by this awakening is not a new idea, is not an enrichment of the content of knowledge; it is a raising of knowledge, of cognition, to a higher level, on which everything is endowed with a new brilliance." Elsewhere, in his later work *Riddles of the Soul* (1916), he writes that perceptions—and science is based upon perceptions—are like seeds, let us say wheat. We can either grind up the wheat to make flour and then bread or pasta, or we can allow those seeds to enter our souls and *germinate*. Natural science makes bread; the "mystics" taught the way of cultivating their souls as a garden in which such seeds could sprout and reach their full potential.

"Mysticism" from this point of view is an inner process that can illuminate and transform—make transparent to their higher meaning—outer facts. The fragmented multiplicity of the "dissected" world becomes thereby unified in *meaning*. This is no mean feat. Modern science has given us tremendous amounts of information. It has been singularly poor in giving us meaning. If we are honest we must admit that we look out on a world about which we know a great deal, but which is meaningless to us. It does not speak to us. Think of the indigenous tribes of the Amazon, how when they walk through their forest world they walk through a world of meaning, a *speaking* world—which is why our pharmaceutical companies go to them to find the latest "miracle" drug. Put another way: "Our inner life not only elucidates itself, but also external things." Or, differently again: "What takes place in our inner life is not a mere [private] mental repetition, but a real part of the universal process."

As I said, this is a process of "awakening." The mystics did not look to the divine as something external to be repeated within them, but as something real in them to be awakened. But this awakening of the divine "spark" within and the reality of God as such were not two for them, but one. Angelus Silesius puts it thus: "I know without me God cannot live for a moment; if I were to come to naught, God would have to give up the ghost." And, again, "God cannot make a single worm without me; if I do not preserve it with God, it would fall apart immediately."

In fact, the world *is* falling apart, and it is up to us to preserve it. This little work can give us some insights as to where to begin.

Preface

to the 1923 edition

THE INTENTION OF THIS WORK of more than twenty years ago was to answer the question, Why did a certain form of mysticism clash with the beginning of modern scientific thought during the thirteenth to the seventeenth centuries? I had no intention of writing a "history" of the mysticism then but to answer this specific question. Publications on this subject since the beginning of the twentieth century do not, in my opinion, provide any basis for changing the answer. The work thus remains essentially unchanged.

The mystics discussed here were the last representatives of a means of inquiry and thinking that, in its details, is alien to contemporary consciousness. But the soul attitude at the center of their methods of inquiry does exist in the nature of thoughtful people today. The way those of this soul disposition viewed natural phenomena (before the period discussed here) has almost disappeared; in its place is modern natural science.

Those described in this book were unable to transmit that earlier method of inquiry into the future. It ceased to correspond to the cognitive forces that developed in Europeans after the thirteenth century. What Paracelsus or Jacob Boehme preserved through this kind of research seems to be merely a memory of a past impulse. It is mainly the disposition of soul that remains in thoughtful people. Such people look for an impulse in the soul's own inclinations, whereas before it arose in the soul while observing nature. Many of those inclined toward mysticism today have no desire to kindle mystical experiences in relation to what modern natural science teaches. Rather, they utilize the ideas from the works of that period. In this way, however, they alienate themselves from present trends.

It might seem as though contemporary knowledge of nature, in its true nature, fails to reveal a way that the soul can find, through mystical contemplation, the light of spirit. Why are mystically inclined souls satisfied with Eckhart, Boehme, and others but not with the book of nature, insofar as it has been opened by knowledge for us today? It is true that, as this book of nature is discussed today, it cannot for the most part lead to a mystical soul nature. This work tries to show that this kind of discussion is unnecessary. I have attempted to show this by speaking of those spirits who, in the soul mood of old mysticism, developed a way of thinking that can incorporate newer knowledge.

Nicholas of Cusa was such a person. In such people it becomes apparent that modern natural science, too, has a capacity for mystical intensification. Nicholas of Cusa would be able to relate his thinking to this science. In his time one could have discarded the old means of inquiry while retaining the mystical disposition and accepting (had it existed) modern natural science. But, if it is strong enough, whatever the human soul finds compatible with a way of inquiry, it must also be able to remove from it.

I wanted to describe the characteristics of medieval mysticism to show how it developed into a mysticism independently of its native soil—the old way of conceiving things. It cannot preserve itself, however, because it now lacks the spiritual impulse that it had in earlier times through its connection with inquiry.

This brings us to the thought that we must look for the aspects of more recent research that lead to mysticism. From this inquiry we can regain the spiritual impulse that does not stop at the darkly mystical and emotional inner life but rises from mystical beginning to knowledge of spirits. Medieval mysticism atrophied because it lost the substratum of inquiry that directs the faculties of the soul upward to the spirit. This book tries to provide a stimulus for extracting the forces directed toward the spiritual world from more recent inquiry, when understood properly.

RUDOLF STEINER
Dornach, Switzerland
Autumn 1923

Introduction

Mystics, Natural Science & the Modern World

THERE ARE MAGIC FORMULAS that have continued to act in new ways throughout the history of ideas over the centuries. In Greece, one such formula—*know thyself*—was considered to be an oracle of Apollo. Such phrases seem to contain within them an infinite life. They may be encountered along the most diverse paths of spiritual life. As one advances and comes to understand all phenomena, the meaning of such formulas becomes deeper. There are times during our meditations and thoughts, they flash like lightning, illuminating our whole inner life. At such times there arises in us the sense that we perceive the heartbeat of humanity's development. How intimate we feel with people of the past when one of their sayings reveals the feeling in us that they, too, have experienced such moments! We have the feeling that we are developing an intimate relationship with those individuals. We become intimately acquainted with Hegel, for example, when we encounter these words:

> One may say that such things are the abstractions we behold when we allow philosophers to dispute and quarrel and decide matters one way or another in our studies; they are abstractions made of mere words. No! Absolutely no! They are acts of universal spirit and, consequently, of fate. In this way philosophers are closer to the master than those who feed on crumbs of the spirit. They read or write the orders from on high in the original—it is their function to take part in writing

them. The philosophers are the mystics who were present at the act in the innermost sanctuary and who participated in it.[1]

When Hegel said this, he experienced one of those moments I described. When he made these statements he had reached the end of Greek philosophy in his historical analysis. Here he showed that neo-Platonic wisdom (which he speaks of at this point) had been illuminated in him like a stroke of lightning. At the moment of that illumination, he became intimate with spirits such as Plotinus and Proclus, and we become intimate with him as we read his words.

We also become intimate with the solitarily meditating vicar in Zschopau, M. Valentinus Wigelius (Valentin Weigel), when we read his words:

> We read in the works of old sages the useful proverb *know thyself*, used primarily in reference to worldly behavior—for example, "Look well at yourself, what you are"; "Search in your heart"; and "Judge yourself, do not censor others." Although, as I say, it is used in human life with respect to behavior, nevertheless the saying *know thyself* may be well-applied to both a natural and a supernatural understanding of humanity. People should look not only at themselves and think of how they should act toward others but also understand their inner and outer nature in spirit and nature—from which they come, are made of, and are intended for.[2]

From his own points of view, Valentin Weigel thus arrived at insights that were summed up for him in the oracle of Apollo.

A similar road to understanding, and the same position with respect to the proverb *know thyself*, can be ascribed to a succession of

---

1. *Lectures on the History of Philosophy* (1887).
2. From his booklet "Know Thyself" (1578). Valentin Weigel (1553–1588), a mystical writer, developed Paracelsist and alchemical ideas. His ideas influenced Jacob Boehme, and other German Protestant mystics of the 17th century. Most of his writings were published after his death, when a small group of Weigelians promoted his ideas, and some texts were issued in his name, pseudonymously.

penetrating spirits, beginning with Meister Eckhart and ending with Angelus Silesius, a group to which Valentin Weigel belongs. Common to these spirits is a strong feeling that a sun rises in human self-knowledge, illuminating something beyond the incidental, individual personality of the beholder. What Spinoza realized in the ethereal height of pure thought—that "the human soul has sufficient knowledge of the eternal, infinite nature of God—lived in them as direct perception. For them, self-knowledge is the path to this eternal and infinite nature. It was clear to them that self-knowledge, in its true form, endows human beings with a new sense. That sense opens a world to humanity that cannot be attained without this sense, just as the world of the physically sighted is unavailable to the blind.

It would not be easy to find a better description of the importance of this new sense than that given by Fichte in his 1813 Berlin lectures:

> Imagine a world of people who are born blind and know only the objects and their conditions that exist through touch. Go to them and speak of colors and other conditions that exist only for our eyes via the medium of light. What you say to them will be nothing, and it is better if they say so, because in this way you will soon see your mistake, and if you cannot open their eyes it will end such useless talk. If, for some reason, they wish to give meaning to your teaching, they would be able to understand it only through their knowledge gained by touch. They will want to *feel* the light, colors, and other visible qualities; they will believe that they feel them and, within the realm of touch, will invent something they name *color* and deceive themselves with it. They will then misunderstand and turn things around and misinterpret them.[3]

---

3. Johann Gottlieb Fichte (1762–1814), German philosopher and exponent of transcendental idealism; he emphasized self-activity of reason. Originally an ardent follower of Kant, he presented a "perfected" Kantian epistemology in which he connected practical reason with pure reason.

We could say something similar about the efforts of those discussed in this book. They viewed self-knowledge as the opening of a new sense. To them, this sense leads to insights that do not exist for those who do not perceive the nature of self-knowledge that differentiates it from all other kinds of knowing. Those to whom this sense is not accessible think that self-knowledge arises somewhat the same as knowledge does through the ordinary senses or through some other external agent; to them, "knowledge is knowledge." In the one case, however, the object is in the outer world, and, in the other, within our souls. They hear only words—or at best, abstract thoughts—where those who look more deeply see the essence of inner life: namely, in the dictum that the object is outside ourselves for all other kinds of knowing, whereas self-knowledge allows us to stand within the object; that every other object comes to us as complete and closed off, whereas, within our self we actively, creatively weave what we observe within.

This explanation may seem like it is mere words, even trivia, but when understood properly, it can appear as a higher light that illuminates all other knowledge in a new way. Those who see this explanation as mere words are in the same position as the blind, to whom one might say, "There is a brilliant object." Such a person hears the words, but the brilliance is nonexistent. One can gather in oneself all of the knowledge of a period; but if one fails to perceive the significance of self-knowledge, all knowledge is blind in the higher sense.

Independent of us, the world lives for us because it communicates itself to our spirit. What is communicated to us must be expressed in a language we understand. A book would be meaningless for us if its contents were to be presented in an unknown tongue. In the same way, the world would be meaningless if it did not speak to us in our own language. The same language that reaches us from the realm of objects we also hear in ourselves, but then it is we who are speaking. It is only a matter of listening properly to the transformation that occurs when we close our perception to external objects and listen only to that which sounds within us. It is for this listening that the new sense is necessary. If it is not awakened, we think that in the communications about us we perceive only communications about an object external to us; we are of the opinion that there is something hidden somewhere that speaks to us in the same way as do external objects. If we have the new sense, we know that its perceptions are quite different from those that refer to external objects. We know that this sense does not separate itself from that which it perceives, as the eye detaches itself from the object it sees, but that it can completely incorporate the object within itself.

If I see an object, the object remains outside me. If I perceive myself, I come into my own perception. A person who looks for some part of the self outside of what is perceived shows that the essence of what is perceived has not become apparent. Johannes Tauler aptly expressed this truth: "If I were a king and did not know it, I would not be a king."[4] If I do not become clear to myself through self-perception, then I do not exist for myself. But when I become clear to myself, *I possess myself through perception in my most fundamental nature. No part of me remains beyond my perception.* Fichte strongly points to the difference between self-perception and all other kinds of perception:

> *It would be easier to convince most people to consider themselves a piece of lava on the moon than a self.* Those who are not in agreement with their self in this sense will not understand any comprehensive philosophy nor do they need one. Nature, whose machine they are, will lead them without their participation in everything they must do. To philosophize, one must be independent, and independence is granted only by one's self. We should not desire to see without eyes, but neither should we assert that it is only the eye that sees.[5]

---

4. Johannes Tauler (1300–1361) was a German mystic, preacher, and member of the Dominican Order. He was expelled from Strassburg and settled in Basel; he was largely influenced by Meister Eckhart and became one of the major mystics of the Rhineland. He stressed practical mysticism over speculation, and his sermons were highly regarded by Martin Luther.

5. J. G. Fichte, *Grundlage der gesamten Wissenschaftslehre* (Berlin, 1812–13).

To perceive oneself, therefore, means to *awaken* the self. Through knowing, we connect the nature of the object with our own nature. The communications bestowed by the outer world through our language become aspects of our self. What confronts me is no longer separate from me when I know it. The aspect of it that I can assimilate is incorporated into my own nature. When I awaken my own self, when I perceive what is within me, I also awaken to a higher existence all that I have incorporated into my nature from outside. The light that falls on me as I awaken also falls on those things of the world that I have assimilated. A light flashes in me, and it illuminates me and, with me, everything I know of the world. All that I know would remain blind knowledge if not for this light falling on it. I could penetrate the whole world with my knowledge, but it would not become what it must within me if knowledge is not awakened to a higher existence within me.

What I add to things through awakening is not a new idea, and it does not enrich the meaning of my knowledge. Rather, it raises knowledge to a higher level that endows everything with new brilliance. As long as I do not raise my cognition to this level, in the higher sense all knowledge remains worthless to me. Things exist without me, too; they contain their own being. What does it mean when I connect another spiritual existence that echoes things within me to the existence of what remains outside me? If it were merely a matter of repetition, this would be pointless. It is a matter of duplication only until I awaken the spirit of what I take into myself to a higher existence within me. When this happens, I have not reproduced the nature of something within me but caused it to be reborn on a higher level.

When I awaken my self, a spiritual *rebirth* of things in the world takes place. In that rebirth, things manifest qualities they had not possessed previously. There, outside, is a tree. I take it into my mind. I shine my inner light on what I have apprehended. Within me, that tree becomes more than it is externally. The part that enters through the portal of the senses is received into spirit; the tree's counterpart as idea is within me. This says infinitely more about the tree than the external tree can tell me. The tree's *nature* shines on it only from me. The tree is now no longer the isolated being it is in external space. It becomes a part of the spiritual world as a whole within me. It combines its meaning with other ideas in me. It becomes a part of the whole world of ideas that embraces the vegetable kingdom; it is further integrated into the evolutionary scale of every living thing.

I could cite another example. Imagine, for example, that I throw a stone horizontally. It moves in an arched path and, after awhile, falls to the ground. In successive moments I see it at different locations. After some reflection, I arrive at the conclusion that, during its movement, the stone was subjected to various influences. If its only influence had been the impulse I gave to it, it would fly in a straight line forever with no change in velocity. But the Earth influences it as well through attraction. If I had simply let go of the stone without giving it an impulse, it would have fallen vertically to the Earth. While falling, its velocity would have constantly increased. The reciprocal action of these two influences produces what I actually see.

But what if I were unable to separate these two influences mentally and reconstruct what I see by combining them according to certain laws, the matter would remain only what was visible. That form of observation would be spiritually blind, merely a perception of the stone's successive positions. In fact, however, matters do *not* remain there. The whole process occurs twice—once outside where my eye sees it, then in my mind, which allows the whole process to repeat before my mind's eye. My inner sense must be directed toward the mental process, which is not seen by my eye, and must realize that I awaken the mental aspect of that process with my own forces. One can again cite a saying of Fichte that makes this clear:

> The new sense is the sense for the spirit. It is a sense for which *only* spirit exists and nothing else; for which the other (given) existence also assumes the manner of spirit, becoming transformed into it; and for which, as a result, existence in its own

right has actually disappeared.... This sense has been used for seeing as long as humankind has existed. Everything great and excellent in the world, and which alone makes humanity endure, originates in the visions of this sense. But it was not true that this sense saw itself as different from and in opposition to the other, ordinary sense. Rather, the impressions of those two senses became fused; life split into these two halves without a unifying bond.[6]

That unifying bond is created because the inner sense perceives spirit, which it awakens through its communication with the spirituality of the outer world. Consequently, the aspect of things we take into our spirit no longer appears as a meaningless duplication. In contrast to what external perception can impart, it emerges as something new. The simple process of throwing a stone as well as my perception of it are seen in a higher light once I clarify the task of my inner sense for myself in this matter. To intellectually combine the two influences and their characteristic actions, I need all of the meaning I gained by perceiving the flying stone. Thus I *use* the mental meaning already stored within me when confronted by something in the external world. This process of the external world is integrated into the preexisting meaning. In essence, this process reveals itself as an expression of this meaning. Through the comprehension of my inner sense, I can see the relationship between the meaning of this sense and things in the external world.

Fichte could say that, without comprehending this sense, the world splits into halves for me—things outside and their images within. Those halves are united when the inner sense understands *itself* and realizes the kind of light it shines on the outer world through cognition. Fichte could also say that this inner sense sees *only* spirit. It sees how spirit illuminates the sensory world by integrating it into the world of spirit. The inner sense allows external,

---

6. *Einleitungvorlesungen in die Wissenschaftslehre, die transzendentale Logik und die Tatsachen des Bewußtseins* (Berlin, 1812).

sensory existence to arise within it as a higher spiritual essence. An external object is completely known when there is no part of it that has not experienced a spiritual rebirth in this way. Every external thing is thus integrated with spiritual meaning, which, when comprehended by the inner sense, participates in the development of self-knowledge. The spirit of a thing enters the world of ideas completely through illumination from within, as does our own self. This explanation contains nothing that can be proved logically, nor is this necessary. It is simply a result of inner experiences. Those who deny its claim merely reveal that they lack such inner experience. It is pointless to dispute such a matter with them just as it would be to dispute color with a blind person.

One should not say, however, that such inner experience is possible only through the gifts of a chosen few. It is a quality common to everyone. Anyone who does not reject it can take the path to its attainment, but such rejection is not unusual. One always has the feeling when encountering objections in this vein that it is not a question of not being able to acquire inner experience but a matter of blocking one's access to it with a multiplicity of logical chimeras. It is almost like looking through a telescope and seeing a new planet and still denying its existence, because *calculations* do not indicate a planet in that particular location.

At the same time, most people definitely feel that there is more to outer nature than is given through the ordinary senses and analysis. They think that everything else must also exist in the outer world, as do the objects of external perception themselves. All that should be apprehended with the inner sense and on a higher level—that is, the object perceived and comprehended with the intellect—is displaced into the outside world to be considered inaccessible and unknown. People speak of limits of knowledge that prevent us from knowing the "thing in itself." People speak of the unknown "essence" of things and never acknowledge that this essence becomes clear when our inner sense lets its light fall upon them.

An especially revealing example of the mistake buried in this attitude was furnished in 1876 by scientist Du Bois-Reymond in his well-known speech, "Ignorabimus."[7] According to him, we should limit ourselves to seeing manifestations of "matter" in natural processes. We cannot know anything about the nature of matter itself. He asserts that we can never get to the point where matter "haunts" space. But the reason we cannot get to that point is because nothing at all can be found there. Those who agree with Du Bois-Reymond think that any understanding of nature points to something else that understanding itself cannot provide. Du Bois-Reymond does not, however, wish to take the path that leads to somewhere else—that is, to inner experience. Consequently, he is helpless when confronted by the problem of matter as though it were a dark secret. For those who take the path of inner experience, phenomena is reborn; whatever remains a mystery for outer experience becomes clear.

Thus, inner human life lights up not only itself but outer reality as well. From this perspective, an infinite vista opens before human knowledge. Within is the glow of a light whose luminosity is not confined to the interior. It is a sun that illuminates *all of* reality at once. Something appears within us that unites us with the world as a whole. We are no longer merely a single, accidental person, no longer a particular individual. The whole world reveals itself within us and discloses its own interrelationships. It shows us how we, as individuals, are connected to it. Knowledge of the world is born from self-knowledge. Our own limited individuality assumes its spiritual place in the grand, interconnected web of the world because something comes to life within us that reaches beyond our individuality and embraces everything in which our individuality participates.

Thinking that does not use logical prejudices to block its own path to inner experience will always come to recognize the essential nature acting within us. This essential nature connects us with

---

7. Emil Heinrich Du Bois-Reymond (1818–1896), German physiologist and professor in Berlin known especially for his investigations of "animal electricity," physiology of muscles and nerves, and metabolic processes.

the whole world because through it we overcome the contrast of inner and outer in relation to ourselves. Paul Asmus (1842–1876), a clear-sighted philosopher who died young, comments on this situation:

> We can become clearer about this matter through an example. Imagine a piece of sugar; it is round, sweet, impenetrable, and so on. These are qualities we all understand. There is only one thing that seems to be completely different and beyond our understanding. It is so different from us that we cannot penetrate it without losing ourselves; our thought timidly recoils from the mere surface of it. This one thing carries all these qualities and is unknown to us. It is the very essence that is the innermost self of that object. Hegel correctly says that the whole meaning of our idea is related to this unfathomable subject only coincidentally, and that we qualify this essence without really getting to the bottom of it. Since we do not know this essence itself, such qualifications ultimately have no real objective value, being only subjective.
> In comprehending thinking, however, we do not encounter an unknowable subject whose qualifications are only accidental; *rather, the objective subject falls within the concept.* If I comprehend something, it is completely present in my concept. I am at home in the innermost sanctuary of its nature not because it lacks its own essence but because it compels me *through the necessity* of the concept (which appears subjectively in me and objectively in it) to *re*think its concept. As Hegel says, this *re*thinking reveals to us that just as this is our subjective activity, *it is at the same time the true nature of the object.*[8]

Only those who can also illuminate the processes of thinking with the light of inner experience can speak in this way.

---

8. Paul Asmus, *Das Ich und das Ding an sich* ("The I and the thing in itself," Halle, 1873).

Beginning from different points of view in *Intuitive Thinking as a Spiritual Path*, I have also pointed to the primordial fact of the inner life:

> Without a doubt: in thinking we hold a corner of the world process where we must be present if anything is to occur. And this is exactly the point at issue. This is exactly why things stand over against me so puzzlingly: because I am so uninvolved in their creation. I simply find them present. But in the case of thinking, I know how it is done. This is why, for the contemplation of the whole cosmic process, there is no more primordial starting point than thinking.[9]

For those who view inner experience in this way, the meaning of human knowledge within the context of the whole universal process is clear; it is not an unimportant supplement to the rest of the universal process. It would be unimportant, however, if it only reiterated, as ideas, external existence. But something that does not occur anywhere in the outer world takes place in *understanding;* that universal process is confronted with its own spiritual nature. The universal process would never be complete if that confrontation did not take place. With it, our inner experience is integrated into the objective, universal process.

It is evident that only a life dominated by the inner sense, our highest spiritual life in the truest sense, lifts us above ourselves. Only in this life is the nature of things revealed in facing itself. It is different for the lower faculties of perception. The eye, for example, mediates the perception of an object; it is the scene of a process that, in terms of the inner life, closely resembles any other outer process. My organs are parts of the spatial world like other things, and their perceptions are temporal processes like others. And their nature becomes apparent only when submerged in inner experience.

---

9. *Intuitive Thinking as a Spiritual Path: A Philosophy of Freedom*, p. 41.

Consequently, I live a double life. I live the life of a thing among things; it exists in its corporeality and through its organs perceives what exists outside that corporeality. And I live a higher life above this one; it knows of no inside and outside and extends over both the external world and itself. I must therefore say that at one moment I am an individual, or limited I, and at another I am a universal I.

This, too, Paul Asmus has put into appropriate words:

> When we submerge ourselves in something else we call it "thinking." In thinking, the I has fulfilled its concept; it has surrendered its separate existence. Therefore, in thinking, we find ourselves in a realm that is the same for everyone, because the principle of isolation (which is the nature of the relationship between the I and what is different from it) has disappeared into the activity of the I suspending the its separateness. There is only *I-being common to all.*[10]

This is exactly what Spinoza has in mind when he stated that the highest activity of cognition proceeds "from an adequate idea of certain attributes of God to an adequate knowledge of the essence of things."[11] This advance is simply the illumination of things by the light of inner experience. Spinoza describes the life of this inner experience in glorious colors:

> The highest virtue of the mind is to know God, or to understand things by the third kind of knowledge, and this virtue is greater in proportion as the mind knows things more by the said kind of knowledge: consequently, those who know things through this kind of knowledge pass to the summit of human perfection and are, therefore, affected by the highest

---

10. *Die indogermanischen Religionen in den Hauptpuniten ihrer Entwicklung*, (The Indo-European religions in their main points of development), vol. 1.
11. Spinoza, *Ethics*, part 5, proposition 25.

pleasure, such pleasure being accompanied by the idea of themselves and their own virtue. Thus, from this kind of knowledge arises the highest possible acquiescence. (*Ibid.*, part 5, proposition 27)

Those who comprehend things in this way transform themselves within, because at such moments the separate I is absorbed by the cosmic, universal I. Cosmic beings do not manifest as subordinate to a separate, limited individual; they appear to themselves. At this level there is no longer a difference between Plato and me; what separates us belongs to a lower level of cognition. We are separated only as individuals; universal nature acting in us is one and the same. One cannot dispute this fact with a person who has not experienced it. Such a person will always insist that Plato and I are two. One cannot prove this dichotomy that all multiplicity is reborn as unity in the development of the highest level of knowing; it must be *experienced*. Paradoxical as it may sound, it is true. The idea that Plato represented to himself and the same idea that I represent to myself are not two ideas. They are one and the same idea. These ideas do not exist separately—one in Plato's head and the other in mine. Instead, in a higher sense, Plato's head and mine interpenetrate; all heads that grasp the same single idea interpenetrate. This unique idea exists only once. It is there, and the heads all transport themselves to one and the same place to contain this idea.

The transformation that takes place in the whole character of people when they adopt this view is shown beautifully in the Bhagavad Gita, the ancient Sanskrit epic. Wilhelm von Humboldt said that he thanked his destiny for allowing him to live long enough to become acquainted with this work.[12] The Inner Light says in this poem:

---

12. Wilhelm von Humboldt (1767–1835) was a German philologist and diplomat to Rome. He was a pioneer in ethnolinguistics, particularly in his study of the Basque language, which has no known affiliation with other languages.

A portion even of me, which becoming an immortal living being in the world of living beings, draws together the senses with mind as the sixth existing in Nature. When the Lord [the soul] acquires a body, and when it departs from it, it takes these senses and goes, like the wind taking scents from their receptacle. It presides over ear, eye, touch, taste, smell, and also the mind, and uses the objects of the senses. When it gets up or stays or enjoys in company with the constituents, the bewildered perceive it not; they who have the eye of knowledge perceive it.[13]

So strongly does the Bhagavad Gita point to human transformation that it says of sages that they can no longer err or sin. If they seem to err, they must illuminate their thoughts or actions with a light in which what seems like sin to ordinary consciousness no longer appears as such. "One whose nature has not the thought of I and whose intellect is not stained, even though one slays all these worlds, slays not nor is bound" (ibid., 18:17). This indicates the same basic disposition of the soul, springing from the highest cognition. Spinoza, after describing it in his *Ethics*, pours out these captivating words:

> I have thus completed all I wished to set forth touching the mind's power over the emotions and the mind's freedom. Whence it appears, how potent are the wise, and how much they surpass the ignorant, who are driven only by lusts. For the ignorant are not only distracted in various ways by external causes without ever gaining the true acquiescence of their spirit, but moreover live, as it were, unaware of themselves, God, and things, and as soon as they cease to suffer, they cease also to be. Whereas the wise, insofar as they are regarded as such, are scarcely disturbed at all in spirit, but, being conscious of themselves, God, and things, through a certain eternal

---

13. Bhagavad Gita, 15:7–10, E. J. Thomas, trans.

necessity, never cease to be but always possesses true acquiescence of spirit. If the way I have pointed out as leading to this result seems exceedingly hard, it may nevertheless be discovered. It must be hard, since it is so seldom found. If salvation were readily available and could be found without great labor, how could it possibly be neglected by almost everyone? All things excellent, however, are as difficult as they are rare. (*Ethics*, part 5, proposition 42)

Goethe outlined the perspective of the highest knowledge most significantly: "If I know my relationship to self and the outer world, I call it *truth*. Thus everyone can have their own truth, and it remains the same truth" (*Verses in Prose*). Everyone has their own truth, because each person is an individual, distinct being compared with others. Those other beings act upon the individual through the organs. From a particular point of view, where one is placed, and according to the nature of that person's faculty of perception, one's own truth develops through communication with things. An individual achieves a relationship to things. Then, when one attains self-knowledge, coming to know one's relationship to self, the particular truth dissolves into the general truth, and this general truth is the same for everyone.

Those who possess a deeper nature view an understanding of the suspension of the individual in a personality—suspending one's I in favor of the universal I—to be the primordial mystery of life revealed within the human being. Goethe also found an apt expression for this: "And so long you that do not have this: Die and become! You are only a cloudy guest on dark earth" ("Blessed Longing").

What takes place in the human inner life is not a mental reiteration but an actual part of the universal process. The world would not be what it is if it were not active in the human soul. And if one calls the highest attainment of the human being the "divine," then one must also say that the divine is not something external to be recapitulated as an *image* in the human spirit. Rather, one must say that the divine is *awakened* within the human being. Angelus Silesius found an appropriate way of saying this: "I know that *without me* God cannot live for a moment; if I come to nothing, he must give up the ghost." He goes on to say, "God cannot make a single worm without me; it would immediately fall apart if I did not preserve it with him."[14] Such an assertion can come only from one who suggests that there is something in the human being that is needed for the existence of an external being. If all that belongs to the "worm" could exist without the human being, it could not be said that the worm would "fall apart" without the human being to preserve it.

In self-knowledge, the innermost core of the world comes to life with spiritual meaning. For the human being, the experience of self-knowledge means acting within the core of the world. Those who are imbued with self-knowledge also naturally conduct their own actions in the light of self-knowledge. Typically, human action is determined by *motives*. It was stated correctly by the poet and philosopher Robert Hamerling:

> It is true that people can do what they will, but they cannot will what they will, because the will is determined by *motives*; they cannot will what they will. Let us examine these words more closely. Is the meaning they convey rational? Would free will thus consist of the ability to will something without motive or reason? But what does it mean to will if not to *have a reason* for one's preference to do or aspire to one thing rather than another? To will without cause or motive would mean to will *without willing it*. Motive as a concept is inseparably related to that of willing. Without a definite motive, the will is an empty *capacity*; only motive makes it active and real. It is indeed correct to say that the human will is not free insofar as its direction is always determined by the strongest motive.[15]

---

14. *The Cherubinic Wanderer*, vol. 1, verses 8, 96.
15. *Die Atomistik des Willens, Beiträge zur Kritik der modernen Erkenntnis*, vol. 2 (The atomistic nature of the will: contributions to a criticism of modern knowledge); Robert Hamerling (1830–1889), born Rupert Hammerling, Austrian poet and school teacher.

For every action that does not take place in the light of self-knowledge, the motive, the cause of the action, must be felt as a compulsion. It is a different matter when the cause falls within the bounds of self-knowledge. Thus, the cause becomes part of the self. The will is no longer determined but determines itself. Conformity to the laws and motives of willing no longer dominate the one who wills; they are no different than the willing itself. To illuminate one's actions with the light of self-observation means to overcome all coercion of motives. In this way, the will places itself within the realm of freedom.

Not all human actions are characterized by freedom. The only free actions are those inspired completely by self-observation. Because self-observation lifts the individual I to the universal I, free action arises from the universal I. The old question of whether the will of the human being is free or subordinated to a general, unalterable necessity is not the real question. Actions performed by a person as an individual are not free; the only free actions are those performed by a person after spiritual rebirth. It is not a question of whether people in general are free or not free; they are both. They lack freedom before their rebirth, and they can gain freedom through such a rebirth. Individually, the upward evolution of humanity involves transforming unfree willing into one that has the character of freedom. Those who have come to understand the principle behind their actions as being their own have overcome the compulsion of that lawful principle and, with this, their own lack of freedom. Freedom is not a given fact of human existence; rather, it is a goal.

In free action, a person resolves a contradiction between the world and self. People's actions become the acts of universal existence. They have a sense of being in complete harmony with this universal existence. Every dissonance between self and other is seen as the result of a not quite awakened self. But it is the destiny of self that it finds contact with that universe only by first being separated from it. People would not be human if they could not be distinguished as individualities apart from everything else. But they would not be human in the highest sense if, as distinct I-beings, they did not raise out of themselves to the universal I. Above all, it is characteristic of human nature that it should overcome a contradiction that is intrinsic to it to begin with.

People who limit spirit to intellectual logic may feel their blood chilled by the thought that things should experience spiritual rebirth. They compare a fresh, living flower outside, in all the fullness of its colors, to a cold, pale, diagrammatic thought of that flower. They become especially uncomfortable at the idea that people who are motivated to act out of solitary self-knowledge are freer than those who are spontaneous and naïve and act on immediate impulses and the fullness of their nature. To one who sees only the onesided, logical aspect, those who are submerged within appear to be a walking demonstration of concepts, a phantom, compared to those who remain within the natural individuality.

One hears such arguments about the spiritual rebirth of things, indeed, particularly among those equipped with healthy organs for sensory perception and with lively drives and passions, but whose capacity for observation falls short when faced with objects having a purely spiritual nature. Their perception fails the moment they are expected to perceive something that is purely spiritual; they deal only with the husks of concepts, if not empty words. Therefore, when the matter of spiritual significance arises, they maintain a dry, abstract intellect. But for those whose gift for observation in the purely spiritual realm is like that in the sensory realm, life does not inevitably become poorer as it is enriched with spiritual meaning. If I look at a flower, why should its rich colors lose even the smallest amount of freshness if not only my eye sees the colors, but my *inner* sense also sees the spiritual nature of that flower? Why should my personal life become poorer because I do not follow my passions and impulses in spiritual blindness, but instead illumine them with the light of a higher knowledge? The life reflected in spirit is not poorer but fuller and richer.

Addendum (1923):

Only those who see spirit only as a collection of concepts abstracted from sensory perceptions fear the impoverishment of soul through an ascent to spirit. People who lift themselves though spiritual vision to a life that goes beyond the senses in terms of meaning and reality are free of such fear. Sensory existence grows pale only through abstractions; sensory existence appears in its true light for the first time through "spiritual sight" and loses nothing of its sensory richness.

Meister Eckhart

THE CONCEPTUAL WORLD of Meister Eckhart radiates the feeling that things are reborn as higher entities in the human spirit.[1] He belonged to the Order of the Dominicans, as did the greatest Christian theologian of the Middle Ages, Thomas Aquinas.[2] Eckhart admired Aquinas in the fullest sense. This is fully understandable when one examines the whole conceptual framework of Meister Eckhart. He considered himself to be in harmony with the teachings of the Christian church to the same degree that he assumed Aquinas to be. Eckhart did not want to take anything away from the meaning of Christianity or add anything to it. He wanted to

---

1. Meister Johannes Eckhart (also Eckehart, c.1260–1326) was born near Erfurt in Thuringia and in his distinguished career became a professor of theology and took a leading pastoral and organizational role in the Dominican order. Eckhart expounds the mysteries of the spark of the soul, the abyss, the desert, the birth of the Word in the heart, etc. Despite Eckhart's distinction and popularity, in the political and ecclesiastical turbulence of the fourteenth century, he was accused of heresy. Some passages of his work were posthumously condemned as heretical or dangerous, and a shadow was cast over his reputation.
2. Thomas Aquinas (b. Aquino, 1225–1274), Italian philosopher and Dominican who studied under Albertus Magnus; became theological adviser and lecturer to the papal Curia and director of Dominican studies at the University of Naples. He is known for integrating scientific rationalism and Aristotle's naturalism with Christian revelation and faith. He replaced Ibn Rushd (Averrös) as principal interpreter of Aristotle. Pope John XXII canonized Aquinas in 1323, and Pope Pius V proclaimed him doctor of the church in 1567.

produce this content anew in *his* way. It was not among the spiritual needs of a one such as himself to replace old truths with various new ones. He was intimately connected with the meaning transmitted to him. But he wanted to give a new form, a new life, to that meaning. Without doubt, he wanted to remain an orthodox Christian. The Christian truths were *his* truths. Only he wanted to look at them in a different way than had Thomas Aquinas, for instance. Aquinas assumed two sources of knowledge—revelation for faith and reason for inquiry.

Reason understands the laws of things—that is, spirit in nature. It can also raise itself above nature and, in the spirit, grasp from one side the divine essence underlying all nature. But in this way it does not achieve an immersion in the *full* essence of God. A higher truth must meet it halfway. This truth is given in the Scriptures. Scriptures reveal what a human being, unaided, cannot attain. A person must assume the truth of the Scriptures; reason can defend it and can try to understand it as well as possible through its powers of cognition, but reason can never produce truth out of human spirit. Spirit sees not the *highest* truth but a certain cognitive content that has come to the spirit from outside. Saint Augustine declares that within himself he is unable to find the source of what he *should* believe.[3] He says, "I would not believe the Gospel if the authority of the Catholic church did not move me to do so."[4] This is stated in the sense of the Evangelist, who refers us to the external testimony: "That which was from the beginning, which we have heard, which we have seen with our eyes, which we have looked upon, and our hands have handled, of the Word of life.... That which we have

---

3. Saint Augustine of Hippo (b. Tagaste, 354–430) from eastern Numidia was originally a Manichaean. He went to Rome as a teacher of rhetoric and was a professor in Milan. Bishop Ambrose of Milan influenced him, and after a spiritual crisis Augustine was converted to Christianity and baptized in 387. He was ordained a priest in 391 and became bishop of Hippo in 396. He became a champion of orthodoxy against Manichaeans, Donatists, and Pelagians. Augustine is best known for his *Confessions*.
4. Augustine, *Contra epistulam Manichaei quam vocant fundamenti*, 6.

seen and heard declare we unto you, that ye also may have fellowship with us" (John 1:1,3).

Meister Eckhart wishes to impress Christ's words upon us: "It is expedient for you that I go away: for if I go not away, the Comforter will not come unto you; but if I depart, I will send him unto you" (John 16:7). And he explains these words by saying, "It is as though he were to say: 'You have taken too much joy in my *present image*; therefore the perfect joy of the Holy Spirit cannot be in you.'"[5] Eckhart thinks that he is speaking of no God other than the one spoken of by Augustine, the Evangelist, and Aquinas, and yet their testimony of God is not *his* testimony:

> Some people want to look upon God with their eyes, as they look upon a cow, and want to love God as they love a cow. They love God for the sake of external riches and of internal solace, but these people do not love God properly. The foolish believe they should conceive of God as though he stood there, and they here.... But this is not how it is. God and I are one in the act of knowing. (sermons 16, 7)

Such declarations by Eckhart are based on an experience of the inner sense. This experience illumines matters with a higher light. Consequently, he does not think that he needs an *external* light to attain the highest insights:

> A master says that God has become flesh; through this, all are raised and exalted. Let us rejoice that Christ our brother has ascended by his own strength above all the angelic choirs and sits on the right hand of the Father. This master has spoken well, but in truth I do not set great store by it. What good would it do me if I had a rich brother while I remained poor?

---

5. Meister Eckhart, *On Solitude*. The following citations of Eckhart's sermons according to J. Quint & J. Koch, *Meister Eckhart: die deutschen und lateinischen Werke* (Stuttgart, 1936).

> What good would it do me to have a wise brother if I were a fool?... The Heavenly Father brings forth his only begotten Son in himself and in me. Why in himself and in me? I am united with him, and he cannot shut me out. In the same act, the Holy Spirit receives being and arises through me as it does through God. Why? I am in God, and if the Holy Spirit does not take its being from me, neither does it take it from God. I am in no way excluded. (sermons 6, 7)

When Eckhart reminds us of the words of Paul, "But put ye on the Lord Jesus Christ" (Romans 13:14), he wishes to give these words this meaning: Become submerged in yourselves; plunge into self-contemplation, and from the depths of your being God will shine upon you. He will outshine everything for you. You will have found him within yourselves; you will have become united with God's essence. "God has become human so that I might become God" (*On the Kingdom of God*). In his treatise *On Solitude*, Eckhart expresses himself on the relationship of external to internal perception:

> Here you must know that the masters say that in each of us there are two kinds of people. One is called the external human—that is, sensuality; one is served by five senses but acts through the force of soul. The other person is called the inner human—that is, one's interior. Now you must realize that those who love God do not use the faculties of the soul in their external being any more than needed by the five senses. The interior human does not turn to the five senses except as a director and guide. The interior human watches over them so that, in their work, they do not pander to animal nature.

One who speaks as Eckhart does about the inner human being can no longer look only at the external, sensory nature of phenomena. We become aware that this nature *cannot* confront us in any outer, sensory world. We might ask, What do things of the outside world have to do with what you add to them from your spirit? Trust your senses. Only they give you knowledge of the outside world. Do not falsify with spiritual adornment what your senses give you without decoration, in purity, as a picture of the outer world. Your eye tells you the nature of a color; nothing that your spirit apprehends about color is in the color. From Meister Eckhart's perspective, one would have to reply that the senses are physical devices. Accordingly, what they communicate about phenomena relates only to the physical characteristics of things. The physical aspects communicate to me by stimulating a physical process within me.

Color as a physical process of the outer world produces a corresponding physical process in my eye and in my brain. Through it, I perceive the color. But in this way I can perceive in the color only what is physical, the sensory aspects. Sensory perception excludes all those features that are not sensory. It divests phenomena of all that is not sensory in them. If I then proceed to spirit, the ideal meaning, I reestablish only the aspect of phenomena that sensory perception has effaced. Hence, sensory perception does not show me the deepest nature of things; rather it separates me from this nature. Spiritual comprehension, comprehension through the idea, again connects me with this nature. It shows me that within themselves things are of exactly the same spiritual nature as I myself.

The boundary between the external world and me is abolished by spiritual comprehension of the world. I am separated from the external world insofar as I am a sensual being in the sensory world. My eye and the color are two different entities. My brain and the plant are two. But the meaning of the plant and of the color, together with the ideal meaning of my brain and of my eye, belong to a unified ideal entity. This view must not be confused with the widespread anthropomorphizing worldview that asserts external phenomena can be comprehended by ascribing to them qualities of a psychic nature, which are supposed to be similar to the qualities of the human soul. This view states that when another person confronts us externally, we perceive only sensory features. I cannot look *into* my fellow human beings. From what I see and hear, I infer their interior, or soul. Consequently, I never perceive the soul directly. I perceive a soul only within myself. No other person sees my thoughts, my imagining, and my feelings. And just as I have such an inner life beside the life that can be perceived externally, so all other beings must have one too. This is the conclusion of someone who takes the anthropomorphizing worldview.

In the same way, the part of a plant that I perceive externally must be only the outer aspect of an interior, of a soul, which I must add, in my thoughts, to what I perceive. Since only a single inner world exists for me—my own—I can only imagine that the inner world of others is similar to mine. In this way, one reaches a sort of universal animation of all nature (*panpsychism*). This view rests on a misunderstanding of what the developed inner sense really offers. The spiritual nature of an external object, which appears to me within myself, is not added in thought to the external perception any more than is the spirit of another human being. I perceive this spiritual content through the inner sense, just as I perceive the physical content through the external senses. What I call my inner life (in the sense indicated earlier) is by no means my spirit in the higher sense. This inner life is the result of purely sensory processes; it belongs to me only as a totally individual personality, which is nothing but the result of its physical organization.

When I transfer this interior life to external phenomena, I am actually indulging in idle fancy. My personal inner life—my thoughts, memories, and feelings—is part of me because I am a creature of nature with a particular organization, with a certain sensory apparatus, with an individual nervous system. I cannot transfer my *human* soul to phenomena. I could do this only if somewhere I found a similarly organized nervous system. But my individual soul is not the highest spiritual part of me. The highest spiritual part must first be awakened in me by the inner sense. This spiritual part that is awakened in me is one and the same with the spirit in all things. Before this spiritual part the plant appears directly in its own spirituality. I need not endow it with spirituality similar to my own. In terms of this worldview, all talk about the unknown "thing in itself" becomes devoid of meaning; it is precisely the so-called thing in itself that reveals itself to the inner sense.

All discussion about the unknown "thing in itself" stems from the fact that those who speak about it are incapable of recognizing the spiritual essence of the "things in themselves." They think that they recognize only insubstantial shadows and phantoms within themselves—merely the concepts and ideas of things. Nevertheless, since they have an intimation of the "thing in itself," they think that it hides and places limits on the human capacity to know. One cannot prove to those who labor under this belief that they must find that "thing in itself" within themselves, since they never would acknowledge it if one showed it to them. It is simply a matter of acknowledgment. Everything Meister Eckhart says is penetrated by this acknowledgment:

> Consider a simile for this. A door opens and closes on a hinge. If I compare the outer boards of the door to the external human being, then I shall compare the hinge to the inner human being. Now when the door opens and closes, the outer boards move back and forth, while the hinge remains constantly immobile and in no way is changed. And here it is the same. (*On Solitude*)

As an individual creature of the senses, I can investigate things in all directions—the door opens and closes. If I do not let the perceptions of the senses arise within me spiritually, I shall know nothing of their essence—the hinge does not move. In Eckhart's view, the illumination mediated by the inner sense is God's entry to the soul. He calls the light of knowledge that is lit by this entry the "spark of the soul." The place within us where this spark is lighted is "so pure, and so elevated, and so noble in itself that no creature can be in it; only God alone dwells there in his pure divine nature" (sermon 34). Someone who has let this spark light up within no longer sees merely as a human being sees with the external senses and with the logical intellect, which orders and classifies the impressions of the senses. Such a person instead sees how things are in themselves.

The external senses and the ordering intellect separate the individual human being from other things; they create an independent being in space and in time who also perceives other things in space and in time. The human being illuminated by the spark ceases to be an individual being. Such a person annihilates isolation. Everything that creates differences between the individual and things ceases to exist. It can no longer even be presumed that it is the *person* as an individual who perceives. The things, and thus also God, see themselves in the individual. "This spark is God, in such a way that it is united and carries within itself the image of all creatures, image without image, and image above image." Eckhart speaks in the most magnificent words of the extinction of the individual being:

> It must therefore be understood that to know God and to be known by God are the same. We know God and see him in that he makes us see and know. And as the air that illuminates is nothing but what it illuminates, for it shines through, illuminating it—in the same way do we know that we are known and that he causes himself to know us. (sermon 35)

It is on this foundation that Meister Eckhart builds his relationship to God. It is a purely spiritual relationship, and it cannot be formed in an image borrowed from the individual life of the human being. God cannot love his creation as one individual loves another; God cannot have created the world as a master builder constructs a house. All such thoughts disappear in the face of the inner vision. It is in the *nature* of God that he loves the world. A god who could love and also not love is formed in the image of the human individual:

> I say in good truth and in eternal truth and in everlasting truth that into every human being who has gone within, God must pour himself out to the limits of his ability. He must pour himself out utterly and completely, so that he retains nothing

in his life and in his being, in his nature and in his divinity. Everything must he pour out in fruitful fashion. (sermon 34)

The soul *must* find inner illumination when it goes down into its depths. It becomes evident that the communication of God to humankind cannot be thought of in the image of the *revelation* of one human being to another. The latter communication can also be left unmade. People can close themselves off to one another. God *must* communicate himself, in conformity with his nature:

> It is a certain truth that God must seek us, as if all his divinity depended upon it. God can no more do without us than we can do without him. Although we may turn away from God, yet God can never turn away from us. (sermon 49)

Consequently, the relationship of the human being to God cannot be understood as comprehending anything figurative, borrowed from what is individually human. Eckhart realizes that part of the fulfillment of the primordial nature of the world is that it should find itself in the human soul. This primordial nature would be imperfect, even unfinished, if it lacked that component of its framework that appears in the human soul. What takes place in the human being belongs to the primordial nature, and if it did not take place, the primordial nature would be only a part of itself. In this sense, human beings can sense that they are a *necessary* part of the nature of the world. Eckhart expresses this by describing his feelings toward God in the following way:

> I do not thank God for loving me, for he cannot keep from doing so, whether he wants to or not; his nature compels him to it.... Therefore I shall not beg God for something, nor shall I praise him for what he has given me. (sermon 33)

This relationship of the human soul to the primordial nature must not be understood to mean that the soul in its individual character is declared to be one with this primordial nature. The soul, which is entangled in the world of the senses and thus in the finite, does not automatically contain the essence of primordial nature; it must first develop this. It must annihilate itself as an individual being. Meister Eckhart has aptly characterized this annihilation as an *"un-becoming."* "When I reach the depths of divinity, no one asks me whence I come and where I have been, and no one misses me, for here there is an *un-becoming*." (sermon 26)

This relationship is also clearly expressed in this way:

> I take a basin of water, place a mirror in it, and put it under the wheel of the Sun. The Sun casts its luminous radiance on the mirror, and yet it is not diminished. The reflection of the mirror in the Sun is Sun in the Sun, and yet the mirror is what it is. Thus it is with God. God is in the soul with his nature and in his being and his divinity, and yet he is not the soul. The reflection of the soul in God is God in God, and yet the soul is what it is.

The soul that gives itself over to inner illumination recognizes in itself not only what it was before illumination but also what it has become only through this illumination:

> We are to be united with God essentially. We are to be united with God as one. We are to be united with God altogether. How are we to be united with God essentially? This is to be accomplished by seeing and not by being. His being cannot be our being, but it is to be our life.

It is not an already existing life—"being"—that is to be understood in the logical sense; the higher understanding—"seeing"—is itself to become life. Spirit—which belongs to the idea—may be experienced by the seeing human being in the same way as the individual human nature experiences ordinary, everyday life.

From such starting points Meister Eckhart also attains a pure *concept of freedom*. In ordinary life the soul is not free, for it is entangled in the realm of lower causes. It accomplishes that to which it is compelled by these lower causes. It is raised out of the region of these causes by "seeing." It no longer acts as an individual soul. In it is exposed the primordial essence, which cannot be caused by anything except itself:

> God does not compel the will; rather he sets it at liberty, so that it wills nothing but what God himself wills. Spirit can will nothing but what God wills. This is not a lack of freedom; it is the spirit's true freedom. For freedom is this, that we are not bound, that we are free and pure and unadulterated, as we were in our first origin and when we were wed in the Holy Spirit. (sermon 29)

It can be said that the enlightened human being is the entity that determines good and evil from within. Such individuals cannot do otherwise than accomplish the good. They do not serve the good; instead the good lives within them. "The righteous serve neither God nor creatures, because they are free, and the closer they are to righteousness, the more they are freedom itself." What, then, must evil be for Meister Eckhart? It can be described only as acting under the influence of the lower view, the action of a soul that has not passed through the state of un-becoming. Such a soul is selfish in the sense that it wills only *itself*. Only externally could it bring its willing into harmony with moral ideals. The seeing soul cannot be selfish in this sense. Even should it will *itself*, it would still will the mastery of the ideal, for it has made itself into this ideal. It can no longer will the goals of the lower nature, for it no longer has anything in common with this lower nature. It is no compulsion, no deprivation, for the seeing soul to act in the sense of moral ideals:

> For the person who stands in God's will and in God's love, it is a joy to do all the good things God wills and to leave undone all the evil things that are against God. And it is impossible for such a person to leave a thing undone that God wants to have

accomplished. As it would be impossible for one to walk whose legs are bound, so it would be impossible for one to do ill who is in God's will. (sermon 29)

Furthermore, Eckhart expressly protests an interpretation that would see in his view a license to do anything the individual might want. We recognize the seeing human being in the fact that a person no longer wants anything as an individual:

> There are those who say, "If I have God and God's freedom, then I can do whatever I want." They understand these words amiss. As long as you can do anything that is against God and his commandment, you do not have God's love; you can only deceive the world into the belief that you have it.

Eckhart is convinced that for the soul that goes down into its depths, in these depths a perfect morality will appear. There all logical understanding and all action in the ordinary sense have an end, and there an entirely new order of human life begins:

> For everything the understanding can grasp, and everything desire demands, is not God. Where understanding and desire have an end, there it is dark, and there God shines. There that power unfolds in the soul which is wider than the wide heavens.... The bliss of the righteous and God's bliss is one bliss, for when God is blissful the righteous are blissful.

The Friendship with God

THOSE MOVEMENTS OF THE SOUL that are aroused in profound natures by a spiritual path such as that of Meister Eckhart appear most impressively in the lives and works of Johannes Tauler, Heinrich Suso, and Jan van Ruysbroeck.[1] If Eckhart seems to be a man who, in the blissful experience of spiritual rebirth, speaks of the qualities and nature of knowledge as of a picture he has succeeded in painting, then the others appear as wanderers to whom this rebirth has shown a new road. They plan to walk this road, but the end of it seems to them to have been removed to an infinite distance. Eckhart describes the splendors of his picture; they characterize the difficulties of the new road.

---

1. Johannes Tauler (c.1300–1361), German mystic and Dominican. While studying, he met Meister Eckhart in Strasbourg and became one of his disciples. He also knew Heinrich Suso. Because the churches of Strasbourg were closed by the bishop there as the result of a quarrel between Pope John XXII and Emperor Louis IV, Tauler went to Basel, where he associated with leaders of the Friends of God, a popular mystical movement that spread Eckhart's teachings. Tauler's sermons were widely disseminated. They are intellectual appeals to practice detachment from the world and to abandon oneself to the Holy Spirit; they abound in striking analogies and keen observations. Tauler referred to Plato and Proclus whom he believed had passed on the Christian truth in veiled terms, but was guided most of all by Dionysius the Areopagite. On Suso and Ruysbroeck, see footnote on page 65.

One must be very clear about the human relationship to higher knowledge before representing the difference between individuals such as Eckhart and Tauler. People are entangled in the sensory world and its natural laws. They themselves are products of this world. They live because its forces and substances are active in them, and they perceive and judge the world of the senses according to the laws that govern it and them. When people direct their eyes to an object, the object appears as a sum of interacting forces dominated by the laws of nature; the eye itself is a body constructed according to such laws and forces.

The act of seeing takes place in harmony with these laws and forces. If we could attain the utmost limits of natural science, in all likelihood we could pursue the play of natural forces in accordance with natural laws into the highest regions of thinking. But in doing so, we rise above this activity. Is not our position above all mere conformity to natural laws when we survey how we ourselves are integrated into nature? We see with our eyes in conformity with the laws of nature, but we also understand the laws that govern the activity of seeing. We can stand on a higher elevation and survey simultaneously the external world and ourselves in interplay.

Is it not true that there is a nature active within us that is higher than the organic, sensory personality, which acts according to natural laws and with natural laws? In such activity is there still a partition between our inner world and the external world? It is no longer our individual personality that judges here, that gathers insights; rather it is the universal essence of the world, which has torn down the barrier between inner world and outer world and which now embraces both.

As it is true that I remain the same individual in external appearance when I have torn down the barrier, so it is true that, in essence, I am no longer this individual. The feeling now lives in me that the universal nature speaks in my soul, the nature that embraces the whole world and me. Such feelings live in Tauler when he says:

The human being is, as it were, three people: an animal being, according to the senses; a rational being; and, finally, the highest godlike being.... One is the external, animal sensual being; the second is the internal, rational being, with rational faculties; and the third is the spirit, the highest part of the soul.[2]

Eckhart has expressed how this third being is superior to the first and second in these words: "The eye by which I see God is the same eye with which God sees me. My eye and God's eye are one eye and one seeing and one knowing and one feeling." (sermon 96) But in Tauler another sentiment lives alongside this one. He struggles through to a real concept of spirit, and he does not continually intermingle the sensory with the spiritual world, as do false materialists and false idealists. If Tauler, with his way of thinking, had become a scientist, he would have had to insist that everything natural, including the whole human being (the first and the second), could be explained in entirely natural terms. He would never have transferred "purely" spiritual forces into nature. He would not have spoken of a "functionalism" in nature, imagined in correspondence with human examples. He knew that where we perceive with the senses, no "creative thoughts" are to be found. Instead, he was unwaveringly conscious of the fact that the human being is a merely natural being. Since he felt himself to be a curator of the moral life, not a scientist, he saw the contrast that separates this natural aspect of the human being from the "seeing" of God, which arises in a natural way within the natural world, but as something spiritual.

It was just in this contrast that the meaning of life appeared before his eyes. Human beings find themselves to be individual beings, creatures of nature. No science can reveal anything more to them about this life than that they are such creatures. They cannot go beyond the state appropriate to such creatures; they must remain

---

2. Sermons 129, 94; Tauler quotes from Julius Hamberger, *Johann Tauler's Predigten* (Frankfurt, 1864).

within it. And yet their inner life leads them beyond it. They must have confidence in a reality no science of external nature can impart. If they call this nature "existence," they must be able to advance to the view that acknowledges nonexistence as the higher order. Tauler does not seek a god who exists in the sense of a natural force; he does not seek a god who has created the world in the sense of human creations. He recognizes that even the concept of creation of the teachers of the church is only an idealized human form of creating. It is clear to him that God is not found in the same manner as science finds natural processes and natural laws.

Tauler knows that we cannot simply add God to nature in our thoughts. He knows that one who perceives God through the senses does not have any more in that thought than one who has apprehended nature in thought. Consequently, Tauler does not want to "think" God; he wants to think divinely. Knowledge of nature is not *enriched* by knowing God; it is *transformed*. A person who knows God does not know something *different* from the one who knows nature; such a person *knows differently*. One who knows God cannot add a single letter to the knowledge of nature, but through this knowledge of nature a new light shines.

The basic sensations that dominate the soul of a person who looks at the world from such points of view will depend on how this individual regards the experience of the soul brought about by spiritual rebirth. Within this experience, people are completely natural when they see themselves interacting with the rest of nature. And they are wholly spiritual beings when they consider the condition that results from their transformation. It may be said with equal justification, therefore, that the greatest depths of the soul are still natural and that they are at the same time divine. In conformity with his way of thinking, Tauler emphasized the former. No matter how deeply we penetrate our souls, he said, we always remain individual human beings. Nevertheless, universal nature glows in the depths of the individual soul.

Tauler was dominated by the feeling that we cannot detach ourselves from our individuality; we cannot cleanse ourselves of it.

Accordingly, the universal essence cannot appear in its purity within human beings; it can only shine into the depths of the soul. Thus, only a reflection, an image of the universal essence appears. We can transform our individual personality so that it gives back the image of the universal essence; the essence itself does not shine within the human being. From such views Tauler came to the idea of a divinity that never entirely merges with the human world, never flows into it. He even expressly insists upon not being confused with those who declare the interior of the human being to be something divine in itself. He says that the union with God

> is thought by ignorant human beings to occur in the flesh, and they say that they should be transformed into divine nature. This is an incorrect and troublesome heresy. Even in the highest and most intimate union with God, the divine nature and God's essence are high, indeed higher than all height. This leads into a divine abyss, and no creature will ever partake of it. (sermon 72)

Deservedly, Tauler wants to be called a believing Catholic, in the sense of his time and of his vocation as a priest. He is not intent upon confronting Christianity with another point of view. He simply wants to deepen and spiritualize Christianity through his views. He speaks of the contents of Scripture as a pious priest. Nevertheless, in his world of ideas the Scriptures become a means of expression for the innermost experiences of the soul:

> God accomplishes all his works in the soul and gives them to the soul, and the Father brings forth his only begotten Son in the soul as truly as he brings him forth in eternity, neither less nor more. What is brought forth when one says, "God brings forth in the soul"? Is it a similitude of God, or is it an image of God, or is it something else of God? It is neither image nor similitude of God but the same God and the same Son whom the Father brings forth in eternity. It is nothing but the lovely

divine Word, which is the other person in the Trinity. This does the Father bring forth in the soul ... and it is from this that the soul derives such a great and special dignity. (sermon 83)

Tauler viewed the narratives of the Scriptures as the garment in which he would clothe the events of the inner life:

Herod, who drove away the Child and wanted to kill him, is an image of the world, which still wants to kill this Child in the devout person. One should and must flee this world if one wants to keep the Child alive within, because the Child is the enlightened, believing soul of every human being. (sermon 15)

Because Tauler directs his attention to the natural human being, he is less concerned with describing what happens when the higher human being enters into the natural human being than with finding the paths that the lower faculties of the personality must take if they are to be translated into the higher life. As a curator of the moral life, he wants to show the human being the ways to the universal essence. He has absolute faith and confidence that the universal essence will begin to shine in humanity if humanity arranges life to make a place for the divine. But this universal essence can never begin to shine if human beings shut themselves off in their bare, natural, separate personalities. Isolated within themselves, in the language of Tauler, human beings are only a part of the world, individual creatures. The more human beings enclose themselves within their existence as part of the world, the less can the universal essence find a place within them:

If one is to become truly one with God, all the faculties of the inner person must die and become silent. The will must be turned away from even the good and from all willing and must become "without will".... People must escape all the senses, turn all their faculties inward, and become forgetful of everything, including themselves.... The true and eternal word of

God is spoken only in the desert once a person has left behind the self and everything and stands alone, deserted and solitary. (sermon 45a)

When Tauler had reached his highest point, the following question became his central concern: How can people destroy and overcome their individual inner existence, so that they can take part in universal life? For those who are in this situation, their feelings toward the universal essence become concentrated in only one thing—reverence for it, as for the inexhaustible and infinite. Such a person may say, "No matter what level one has attained, there are still higher prospects, still more sublime possibilities." The steps such a person must take are definite and clear; it is equally clear that one can never speak of a goal.

A new goal is only the beginning of a new road. With a new goal, a person has reached a certain degree of development; development itself extends into the immeasurable. At the present level, one can never know what will be achieved at a more distant level. We cannot discern the final goal; we can only trust in the road, in the development. It is possible to arrive at knowledge of everything the human being has achieved. It consists in the penetration of an already existing object by the faculties of spirit. For the higher inner life, such knowledge does not exist. Here the faculties of the spirit must first translate the object itself into existence; they must first *create* an existence for it that is like the natural existence. Natural science examines the development of living beings from the simplest creature to the human being, the most perfect. This development lies completed before us. We understand it by penetrating it with our mental faculties. When development comes, one does not *find* its continuation already exists; we accomplish that development ourselves. We now *live* what we only *knew* at earlier levels. We create objectively, according to our spiritual natures, what we only *re-created* at preceding stages.

The truth does not coincide only with what exists in nature; it embraces both the naturally existent and the nonexistent. This idea completely filled Tauler in all his considerations. We are told that an enlightened layperson, a "Friend of God from the Oberland," led him to this conviction. This involves a mysterious story. There are only conjectures about the place where this Friend of God lived; about whom he was, there are not even conjectures. He is said to have heard much about Tauler's manner of preaching and to have decided as a result to go to Tauler (who was then a preacher in Strasbourg) to fulfill a certain task pertaining to him. The relationship of Tauler to the Friend of God and the influence that the Friend exercised on him are described in a work that is printed together with Tauler's sermons in the oldest editions under the title *Das Buch des Meisters* ("The book of the master"). In this book, the Friend of God (in whom we recognize the same one who entered into a relationship with Tauler) tells of a "master" who has been identified as Tauler himself. He tells how a revolution, a spiritual rebirth, had been brought about in a certain "master" and how this master, when he felt his death approaching, called the Friend to him and asked him to write the story of his "enlightenment." He further asked that the Friend take care that no one should ever discover the identity of the book's subject. He asks this because all the insights that emanate from him are yet not his alone. "For know that God has performed everything through me, poor worm that I am, and thus it is not mine, but God's." (*Das Buch des Meisters*)

A scholarly dispute has developed in connection with this matter, but it is not at all important as far as its essentials are concerned. On the one hand, an attempt has been made to prove that the Friend of God never existed.[3] It is said that his existence was invented and that the books attributed to him in fact originated with someone else (Rulman Merswin). Wilhelm Preger (in his history of German mysticism) has argued in support of his existence, the genuineness of the writings, and the correctness of the

---

3. Heinrich Denifle, *Die Dichtungen des Gottesfreundes im Oberlande* ("The writings of the Friend of God in the Oberland, Berlin, 1880–1881).

facts relating to Tauler. It is not incumbent upon me to illuminate by obtrusive research this human relationship, which one who understands how to read the relevant writings will know full well is to remain a secret.[4]

It is enough to say of Tauler that at a certain stage of his life, a change such as the one I am about to describe took place in him. Here Tauler's personality is no longer in question, but rather a personality "in general." With regard to Tauler, we are concerned only with the fact that we must come to understand the transformation in him from the perspective I will indicate. If we compare his later with his earlier activity, the fact of this transformation is immediately evident. I omit all external circumstances and relate the inner soul processes of the master under the "influence of the layperson." The spiritual disposition of the reader completely determines *who* this layperson and master are. I do not know if my own imagination of them applies to anyone else.

This master instructs his listeners about the relationship between the soul and universal essence. He explains that people no longer feel that the natural, limited faculties of the individual personality are active within them when they descend into the profound depths of the soul. There it is no longer the individual who speaks, but God. The human being there does not see God or the world; God sees himself. The human being becomes one with God. But the master knows that this teaching has not yet come fully to life within him. He thinks it with the intellect, but he does not yet live within it with every fiber of his personality. In this way he teaches about a state that he has not yet fully experienced within

---

4. These relevant writings, among others, are: *Von eime eiginwilligen weltwisen manne, der von eime heiligen weltpriestere gewiset wart uffe demuetige gehorsamme* (Of a self-willed, worldly man who was shown the way to humble obedience by a holy, secular priest, 1338); *Das Buch von den zwei Mannen* (The book of the two men); *Der gefangene Ritter* (The captured knight, 1349); *Die geistliche siege* (The spiritual stairs, 1350); *Von der geistlichen Leiter* (Of the Spiritual Ladder, 1357); *Das Meisterbuch* (The book of the master, 1369); *Geschichte van zwei jungen 15 jährigen Knaben* (Story of two young fifteen-year-old boys).

himself. The description of this state corresponds to the truth, but this truth is worth nothing if it does not acquire life, if it does not take up existence in the real world.

The "layperson," or Friend of God, hears of the master and his teachings. He is not less penetrated with the truth the master utters than is the master himself. But he does not possess this truth as an intellectual idea—he possesses it as the whole force of his life. He knows that one can impart this truth when it is acquired from the outside, without living in its essence in the least. In that case, a person has nothing within, beyond the natural understanding of the intellect.

One then speaks of such natural understanding as though it were the highest truth, identical with the activity of universal essence. This is not so, because it was not acquired in a life already transformed and reborn when it approached this knowledge. The knowledge one attains as a merely natural, human being remains only natural, even if one expresses the main features of the higher knowledge later in words. The transformation must come out of nature itself. Nature, which has developed to a certain stage, must be developed further by life; something new must come into existence through this further development. One must not simply look back upon the development that has already taken place and consider what is *re*-formed in the mind concerning this development to be the highest truth. One must instead look forward to what has not yet been created; this knowledge must be the beginning of new meaning, not an outcome of the meaning of one's previous development.

Nature advances from worm to mammal, from mammal to human being in a real process, not a conceptual one. The human being is not intended merely to repeat this process in spirit. The spiritual recapitulation is only the beginning of a new development, which is also a spiritual reality. Human beings do not just understand what nature has produced; they carry nature further. They transform their understanding into living action. They bring forth the spirit within themselves, and from then on the spirit advances from one stage of development to another, just as nature advances. The spirit initiates a natural process on a higher level.

When one who has understood this evolution speaks about the God who sees himself within the human, this utterance assumes a different character. One attaches little value to the fact that a previously achieved insight has led into the depths of the universal essence; one's spiritual disposition acquires a new character. It continues to develop in the direction determined by the universal essence. Not only is the worldview of such a one different from that of the person who is merely rational, but that one also lives life differently. This person does not speak of the meaning that life already has by virtue of the forces and laws of the world; rather this individual gives a *new* meaning to life.

Rational human beings do not immediately possess within themselves the higher human being that may be born any more than a fish has within itself the mammal that may appear at a later stage of development. If a fish could understand itself and its surroundings, it would believe that its "fishhood" represents the meaning of life. It would say, "The universal essence is like a fish; universal essence sees itself in the fish." The fish might speak in this way as long as it merely holds on firmly to its intellectual understanding. In reality, however, it does not hold on to it. In its actions it goes beyond its understanding. It becomes a reptile and later a mammal. The meaning the fish gives itself goes beyond the sense suggested to it by mere reflection. And this is how it must be for human beings. We give ourselves meaning; we do not stop at what we are and what we find reflected back to us. Understanding leaps beyond itself only when it understands *itself* in the right way. Understanding cannot derive the world from an prefabricated god; it must develop in a direction toward God from a seed.

Those who have come to this understanding prefer not to view God as an external being. They want to treat God as a being who walks with them toward a goal—one that is just as mysterious at the outset as mammal nature is to a fish. They do not want to simply know the hidden or self-revealing, already existing God;

they want to be friends of the divine action and operation, which is superior to both existence and nonexistence. The layperson who came to the master was a "Friend of God" in this sense. Through him the master was transformed from a contemplator of the nature of God into "one who lives in the spirit," one who did not merely contemplate but *lived* in the higher sense. The master no longer simply shared his intellectual concepts and ideas; these concepts and ideas sprang from him as living, true spirit. He no longer merely edified his listeners; he moved them deeply. He no longer plunged their souls within themselves; he led them into a new life. This is related to us symbolically. We are told that, through the effect of one of his sermons, forty people collapsed as though dead.

Another leader into such a new life is represented in a certain work by an unknown author. Martin Luther was the first to bring it to light by publishing it. The philologist Franz Pfeiffer recently reprinted it from a manuscript of 1497, with a translation in modern German facing the original text. The introduction to the work announces its intention and goal: "Here the Frankfurter says exceedingly deep and beautiful things of the consummate life." This introduction is followed by a preface concerning the "Frankfurter," which states:

> What is expressed in this booklet the omnipotent, eternal God has spoken through a wise, judicious, truthful, righteous man, his friend, who was formerly a Teutonic Knight, a priest, and a custodian in the house of the Teutonic Knights in Frankfurt. It teaches many lovely insights into divine truth and especially how one can recognize the true and righteous Friends of God as well as the unrighteous, false, free spirits, who do much harm to the holy Church.[5]

---

5. Franz Pfeiffer, *Theologia deutsch* (Stuttgart, 1855).

"Free spirits" may be taken to mean those who live in a world of ideas like that of the master described earlier before his transformation by the Friend of God. The "true and righteous Friends of God" are those who think in the way of the "layperson."

We can further ascribe to the book the intention of having the same effect on its readers as the "Friend of God from the Oberland" had upon the master. We do not know the author. But what does this mean? We do not know when he was born, when he died, and what he did in ordinary life. It is integral to the way the author wanted to work that the facts of his outer life should remain forever secret. It is not the "self" of this or that human being, born at a certain time, that is to speak to us but the selfhood on the basis of which the "particularity of individualities" first develops (in the sense of the words of Paul Asmus[6]):

> Imagine God receiving unto himself all those who exist now and all those who have ever been, and in them becoming human; and imagine that they, too, become God in him. If this did not also happen in me, my fall and my estrangement would not be remedied until it indeed happened in me as well. And in this restoration and improvement I can and should do nothing but only and purely submit to what is done, so that God alone accomplishes everything within me, and I yield to him and all his works and his divine will. But if I do not want to become transformed and instead cling to attributes of the self—that is, to "my" and "I," to "me" and so on—then God is hindered. He cannot accomplish his work within me, pure and alone and without obstacle. Accordingly, my fall and my estrangement remain unremedied.[7]

The "Frankfurter" does not intend to speak as an individual; he wants to allow God to speak. Of course, he knows that he can do

---

6. Paul Asmus, see page 27.
7. Julius Pfeiffer, *Theologia deutsch*, pp. 11, 13.

this only as an individual personality. But he is a Friend of God—that is, one who does not want to depict the nature of life through contemplation but wants to point out, through the living spirit, the beginning of an avenue of development.

The discussions in the book represent various instructions on how this road is to be attained. The basic idea is that human beings are to cast off everything connected with the belief that they are separate individualities. This idea seems to be carried out only with respect to the moral life; it must also be applied to the life of higher understanding. One must root out in oneself what appears as separateness. Then independent existence ceases; universal life enters us. We cannot possess universal life by drawing it to us. It comes into us when we silence the separate existence within us. We possess universal life least of all when we regard our individual existence as if universal life already reposed within it. It appears in the individual existence only when the individual existence does not claim that it is a distinct entity.

The book calls this claim of individual existence the "assumption" (ibid., pp. 7, 9). Through this assumption, the self makes it impossible for universal life to enter it. The self then puts itself in the place of the whole as a part, as something incomplete:

> The "whole" comprises and embraces all beings. Without and outside this whole, there is no true being. All things have their being in the whole, for it is the essence of all things and is in itself unchangeable and immovable and changes and moves all other things. But the world of divided and incomplete beings arose from the whole (or what it becomes), in the same way as the brilliance or luminosity emanating from the sun or from a light appears as a distinct entity. This entity is called "creature," and none of these separate entities is identical with the whole. *Therefore the whole also is not identical with any of the separate entities.*... When the whole appears, one rejects what is distinct and separate. But when does it appear? I say it is when it is known, felt, and tasted in the soul, insofar as it is

possible. The lack is wholly in us and not in it. Even though the Sun illuminates the whole world, and even though it is as close to one person as to another, one who is blind nevertheless cannot see it. That is not a defect in the sun, but rather in the blind person.... If my eye is to see something, it must be cleansed of, or freed from, all other things.... One might ask, Insofar as the whole is unknowable and incomprehensible for all creatures (and the soul is a creature), how can it be known in the soul? The answer is this: the creature is to be known as *creature*. (ibid., pp. 3, 5, 7)

This is like saying that everything "creature" should be regarded as *creature nature* and as created, and that it should not regard itself as an I with selfhood, which makes knowing it impossible. "In the creature in which the complete is to be known, creatureness, created being, I, selfhood, and so on must be lost and amount to nothing."[8] Thus, the soul must look to itself; there it will find its I-being, or selfhood. If it stops there, it separates itself from the whole. If it regards its selfhood only as something loaned to it, as it were, and obliterates it in spirit, the stream of the universal life, the whole, will seize it:

Let us say that a creature takes on something good, such as being, life, knowledge, insight, capacity—in other words, all that one would call good—and deems that it, as a creature, *is* that attribute or that the attribute belongs to it or is part of it. As long as this happens, such a creature rejects itself.... [There are] two eyes in the created soul of the human being. One has the possibility of looking into eternity, the other of looking into time and into the creature.... People should stand in freedom—without selfhood, "I," "me," "my," and so on—so that they are no more self-seeking and self-determining than if

---

8. The works of the "Frankfurter," chapter 1.

they did not exist. People should also value themselves as if they did not exist and as though someone else had accomplished all their works. (ibid., p. 9, 25, 51, 53)

It must be understood that the concepts that the author of these words articulates through his higher ideas and feelings are those of a devout priest of his time. It is not a matter of the conceptual content but of the direction, not of the ideas but of the spiritual disposition. A person who does not live within Christian dogma (as this author does), but within the concepts of natural science, lends other meanings to those words. But with the other meanings those words point in the same direction. This direction leads to overcoming selfhood through selfhood itself. It is within the self that the highest light shines for the human being. This light gives the right reflection to the world of ideas only when the human being is aware that it is not the light of the self but the universal light of the world. Consequently, there is no more important knowledge than self-knowledge, and at the same time there is none that so completely leads beyond itself. When the "self" knows itself in the right way, it is no longer a self. That particular author expresses it this way:

> For God's nature is without individual aspects and without selfhood and I-being. But the nature and peculiarity of the creature is that it seeks and determines itself and what belongs to it and its particular characteristics. From everything that it does or leaves undone, it wants to receive profit and advantage. But where the creature (or human being) loses its own being and selfhood and goes beyond the self, there God enters with his being and with his selfhood. (ibid., p. 87)

We ascend from a concept of the self in which the self appears as essence to a concept in which we see it as a mere organ where universal essence acts upon itself. In line with the ideas of our book, it is said: "If people can reach the point where they belong as much to God as their hands belong to them, they can rest content and seek no further" (ibid., p. 233). This does not mean that one being should stop at a certain point in development. When one has come as far as these words indicate, one should no longer pursue investigations about the meaning of the hand, but instead *use* the hand so that it serves the body to which it belongs.

"Genius of soul" would be the proper way to describe the spiritual disposition of Heinrich Suso and Jan van Ruysbroeck.[9] Their feelings were drawn by an impulse resembling instinct toward the same point to which Eckhart's and Tauler's feelings were led through a higher life of ideas. Suso's heart turns ardently toward a primordial essence that embraces the individual human being as well as the whole remaining world and in which, forgetting himself, he wants to be absorbed like a drop of water in the great ocean. He speaks of this yearning for the universal essence not as something he wants to grasp in his thoughts. He speaks of it as a natural impulse that intoxicates his soul with a desire for the annihilation of his separate existence and for rebirth in the all-embracing activity of infinite essence:

> Turn your eyes toward this being in its pure simplicity and let go of this or that which only participates in being. Take being alone in itself, which is not mixed with nonbeing. For just as

---

9. Jan van Ruysbroeck, (1293–1381), Roman Catholic mystic, b. Brabant (now in Belgium and the Netherlands). He was an Augustinian canon. In his middle age he retired to a hermitage at Groenendael (near Brussels), where he was prior of a small community. His sanctity and good counsel attracted visitors from afar, and Johannes Tauler and Gerard Groote were among his followers. His influence on Groote was so great that Tauler is considered a forerunner of the Brothers of the Common Life.

Heinrich Suso (c.1295–1366), German mystic and Dominican friar. While studying in Cologne he was influenced by Meister Eckhart, whose writings he defended against charges of heresy. He became a popular preacher associated with Johannes Tauler. At first harshly ascetic, he gradually emphasized detachment rather than mortification as central in the Christian discipline. His mysticism was expressed in terms of the contemporary literary romantic cult of the minnesingers, which gave him the epithet "Sweet Suso." He was beatified in 1831.

nonbeing negates all being, so being in itself is the negation of all nonbeing. A thing that is yet to come about or has already been is not at this moment really existing as being. Now one can know mixed being or nonbeing only by referring them to total being. It is not a divided being of this or that creature, because divided being is all mixed together with some otherness of potency to receive something. Therefore the nameless divine being must be in itself complete being that supports all divided beings with its presence.[10]

Thus speaks Suso in the autobiography he composed with the aid of his disciple Elsbet Stäglin. He, too, was a devout priest and lived fully in the Christian realm of ideas. He lived in it as if it were completely unthinkable for someone with his spiritual direction to live in a different spiritual world. It is also true that one can associate another conceptual significance with his spiritual direction. This is clearly indicated by the way the content of the Christian doctrine becomes an inner experience for him, while his relationship to Christ becomes one between his spirit and the eternal truth, of a purely conceptual, spiritual kind. He wrote *Little Book of Eternal Wisdom*, in which he allowed "eternal wisdom" to speak to its "servant," presumably himself:

> Don't you recognize me? Have you sunk so low? Or are you faint from your immense sorrow? My dear child, it is I, gentle merciful Wisdom, who, while remaining hidden to all the saints in my innermost depths, have opened up wide the abyss of my mercy to receive you and all penitent hearts kindly. It is I, dear Wisdom, who became poor and outcast, so that I might return you to your true dignity. It is I, who suffered a bitter death in order to let you live again. I stand here now pale, bloody, and loving, as I stood on the high gallows of the cross mediating between you and the stern judgment of my Father.

---

10. Heinrich Suso, *The Exemplar: With Two German Sermons*, p. 191.

It is I, your Brother, your Husband. I shall forget everything that you have ever done to me, as though it had never happened, if only you will completely turn to me alone and never again leave me.[11]

As we can see, everything material and temporal in the Christian view of the world has become for Suso a spiritual, ideal process within his soul. From some chapters of the autobiography of Suso, it might appear as if he had let himself be led not by the mere activity of his own spiritual faculties but by external revelations, by spirit-like visions. But he clearly expresses his opinion about this: one attains the truth only by exercise of reason, not through revelation:

I shall also tell you how to distinguish between pure truth and dubious visions originating in sense knowledge. Direct sight of the naked Godhead: this is pure genuine truth without any doubts. And every vision, the more intellectual and free of images it is and the more like this same pure seeing, the nobler it is.[12]

Meister Eckhart also leaves no doubt that he rejects the view that sees the spirit in substantial, spatial forms, in apparitions that can be perceived in the same way as sensory ones. Spirits like Suso and Eckhart are opponents of a view such as that expressed in the spiritualism that developed in the eighteenth century. Jan van Ruysbroeck walked the same paths as Suso.[13] His spiritual road found a spirited opponent in Jean de Gerson (1363–1429), who was for some time chancellor of the University of Paris and played an

---

11. Ibid., p. 221.
12. Ibid., p. 195.
13. Jan van Ruysbroeck's mystical treatises are classics of Middle Dutch literature and Christian mysticism. His works include *The Seven Steps of the Ladder of Spiritual Love* and *The Spiritual Espousals*. He was beatified in 1908.

important role at the Council of Constance.[14] It throws light on the nature of the mysticism cultivated by Tauler, Suso, and Ruysbroeck if one compares it with the mystical endeavors of Gerson, whose predecessors were Richard of St. Victor, Bonaventura, and others.[15] Ruysbroeck himself fought against those whom he counted among the heretical mystics. He believed heretical mystics to be all those who, on the basis of an unconsidered intellectual judgment, hold all things to be the emanation of one primordial essence and who thus see in the world only a diversity and in God the unity of that diversity.

Ruysbroeck did not count himself among those mystics. He knew that one cannot reach the primordial essence by contemplating the things themselves but only by raising from this lower to a higher way of thinking. Similarly, he turned against those who, without further ado, wanted to see a higher nature in the individual human being, in separate existence (in our creatureness). He very much lamented the error that eliminates all differences in the sensory world and says lightly that things merely appear to be different, whereas, in fact, they are all essentially the same.

For a way of thinking such as Ruysbroeck's, this would be the same as if one were to say, "It is of no concern to us that our eyes see trees along an avenue converge in the distance. The fact is that

---

14. By the election of Martin V as Pope (Nov. 11, 1417), the Council of Constance ended the Great Schism but did not have time to reform. The council issued two canons that represented the high points of conciliar thought. The first canon—*Sacrosancta*—declared that the Council of Constance derives its power directly from Christ and that its authority is superior even to that of the See of Rome. The second canon, *Frequens*, called for the frequent invocation of future councils to promote reform. A list of abuses to be addressed was also issued. Later popes largely nullified the intended results, perhaps laying the path to the Reformation.

15. Saint Bonaventura (c.1217–1274), born Giovanni; he became a Franciscan and later a professor of theology in Paris; he was named Bishop of Albano by Gregory X. He was known for his great devotion and wisdom and for revitalizing the Franciscan order; he was canonized in 1482.

they remain equally distant, and so our eyes must adjust to see them correctly." But our eyes do see correctly. The trees do converge owing to a necessary law of nature, and we should not oppose this way of seeing but understand why we see in this way.

Neither do mystics turn away from objects of the senses but accept them as sensory, as they are. And it is clear to them that such phenomena cannot become something else through any intellectual judgment. But in the spirit they go beyond the senses and reason, and only then do mystics find unity. They have an unshakable belief that they can develop to the point of seeing this unity. Therefore they ascribe to human nature the divine spark that can be made to shine within on its own.

It is different with those of Gerson's kind. They do not believe that this shining is intrinsic. For them, what human beings can see always remains an external reality that must approach them outwardly from one side or another.

Ruysbroeck believed that the highest wisdom must become apparent to mystical vision; Gerson believed only that the soul could illuminate the content of an external teaching (that of the church). Gerson saw mysticism as merely having a warm feeling for everything that is revealed in this teaching. To Ruysbroeck, it was a belief that the content of this teaching is also born in the soul. Gerson reproves Ruysbroeck for imagining not only that he possesses the capacity to see the universal essence with clarity but also that an activity of the universal essence manifests itself in this vision.

Gerson simply could not understand Ruysbroeck. They were speaking of two different things. Ruysbroeck has his eye fixed on the life of the soul that lives its god; Gerson sees only a life of the soul that wants to love a god to whom it never will be able to give life. Like so many others, Gerson, too, fought against a foreign idea only because it would not fit his experience.

Addendum (1923):

In my writings, I speak of "mysticism" in various ways. People have claimed to find what seems to them a contradiction in this. This is explained in the annotations to the new edition of my *Theory of Knowledge in Goethe's Conception of the World.*

Cardinal Nicholas of Cusa

NICHOLAS CHRYPFFS OF CUSA was a gloriously shining star in the firmament of medieval spiritual life.¹ He stood on the heights of learning during his time. He produced outstanding work in mathematics, and in natural science he may be described as the precursor of Copernicus, for he believed that the Earth is a moving heavenly body like others. He had broken with the view that the great astronomer Tycho Brahe still held a hundred years later.² Brahe argued against the teaching of Copernicus by saying, "The Earth is a coarse and heavy mass, unsuited for movement. How can Copernicus make a star of it and lead it around in the atmosphere?"³ Nicholas of Cusa, who did not simply embrace the knowledge of his time but developed it further, also had an elevated capacity to

---

1. Nicholas of Cusa (1401–1464), German prelate and philosopher, became cardinal in 1448 and bishop of Bressanone in 1450. He wrote on the supremacy of church councils, experimented in botany, collected manuscripts, and discovered the lost comedies of Plautus. Cusa is near Trèves (or Trier), Germany, in the Rhineland-Palatinate, on the Moselle River, about six miles from Luxembourg.
2. Tycho Brahe (1546–1601), Danish astronomer who helped to establish the Uraniborg observatory on the island of Hven (now Ven). Johannes Kepler (1571–1630) was his assistant under the patronage of Rudolf II in Bohemia. He proved nova was a star, and believed that the five planets revolve around the Sun, all of which revolve around the Earth, which remains stationary. His observations were published by Kepler in the *Rudolphine Tables*.
3. *Opra omnia* (Kassel, 1590).

awaken this knowledge to an inner life. For him, it not only elucidated the external world but also gained for human beings the spiritual life for which they yearned from the most profound depths of their souls.

If we compare Nicholas with such spirits as Eckhart or Tauler, we reach an important conclusion. Nicholas is the scientific thinker whose goal is to rise to a higher view through his research into world phenomena; Eckhart and Tauler are the believing confessors who seek a higher life through the meaning contained in their faith. Nicholas finally reaches the same inner life as Meister Eckhart, but the substance of his inner life is a rich learning process. The full meaning of the difference becomes clear when we consider that for a person who is interested in the various sciences, there is a real danger of misjudging the scope of the paths to knowledge in different fields of learning. Such a person can easily be misled into the belief that there is only one way of knowing and will then either underestimate or overestimate the paths of knowledge that lead to a goal in matters pertaining to the various sciences.

In the one case, people will approach phenomena of the highest spiritual life in the same way as a problem in physics and deal with them in terms of concepts used to elucidate the forces of gravity and electricity. According to whether such people consider themselves to be more or less enlightened, the world becomes a blindly acting mechanism, an organism, the functional construction of a personal God, or, perhaps, a structure directed and penetrated by a more or less clearly imagined "world soul." In the other case, they notice that the particular knowledge of which they have experience is useful only for the things of the sensory world. Then they become skeptics who might say, "We cannot know anything about what lies beyond the sensory world. Our knowledge has limits. When we aspire to the necessities of higher life, we merely throw ourselves into the arms of a faith, untouched by knowledge." For a learned theologian like Nicholas of Cusa, who was at the same time a natural scientist, the second danger was particularly real. In his education he was a product of Scholasticism, the dominant philosophy in the scholarly life of the Church of the Middle Ages, which had been brought to its highest flowering by Thomas Aquinas, the "Prince of Scholastics." This philosophy must be used as a background if one wants to depict the personality of Nicholas of Cusa.

Scholasticism, to a great degree, is a product of human ingenuity. In Scholasticism the logical faculty celebrated its greatest triumphs. One who aims to elaborate concepts in their sharpest and clearest contours should serve an apprenticeship with the Scholastics. It is they who provide the best training for the technique of thinking. They had an incomparable agility in the field of pure thought. It is easy to underestimate what they were capable of accomplishing in this field. In most areas of learning, agility in the realm of thought is accessible to the human being only with difficulty. Most people attain it clearly only in the areas of counting and calculating (arithmetic) and in considering the properties of geometric forms. We can count by adding a unit to a number in our thoughts, without calling sensory images to our help. We also calculate without such images, in the pure element of thought alone. As for geometric forms, we know that they do not completely coincide with any sensory image. In the reality of the senses, there exists no (conceptual) circle. And yet our thinking occupies itself with this circle.

It is more difficult to find conceptual counterparts for objects and processes that are more complicated than numerical and spatial structures. This difficulty has led to the claim, in various fields of investigation, that real knowledge is represented only by that which can be measured and counted. This is decidedly wrong in that it is one-sided, but it seduces many, as often only one-sided ideas can. The truth is that most people are not capable of grasping the purely conceptual when it is no longer a matter of measuring and counting. But someone who cannot grasp the higher realms of life and knowledge resembles a child who has not yet learned to count in any other way than by adding one pea to another. The thinker who said that there is as much true knowledge in any field of learning as there is mathematics in it did not grasp the full truth of the matter. We must require that everything that cannot be measured and counted be treated in the same conceptual fashion as numerical and spatial structures. And this requirement was greatly respected by the Scholastics. Everywhere they sought the conceptual content of things, just as the mathematician seeks it in measuring and counting.

In spite of this accomplished logical skill, the Scholastics attained only a one-sided and subordinate concept of cognition. According to this concept, in the process of cognition the human being produces an image of what is to be grasped. It is quite obvious that with such a concept of cognition, one must place all reality outside cognition. In the process of cognition one cannot grasp a thing itself but only an image of this thing. People also cannot grasp themselves in self-knowledge; what they grasp is only an image of the self. It is quite in the spirit of Scholasticism that someone who is closely acquainted with it says:

> In time people have no perception of the self, the hidden foundation of spiritual nature and life.... They will never be able to look at themselves. Forever estranged from God, they find in themselves only a bottomless dark abyss and endless emptiness. Or else, blessed in God and turning their gaze inward, people find only God, whose sun of grace shines within and whose image is reflected in the spiritual traits of their nature.[4]

Someone who thinks about all knowing in this way has a concept of such knowledge that applies only to the external world. The sensory aspects of reality always remain external to us. We can receive into our perception only sensory images of the world. When we perceive a color or a stone, we ourselves cannot become color or stone in order to know the nature of color or stone. Neither can the color or the stone transform itself into a part of our own nature. Focused as it is on the outer, is a concept of this form of knowledge exhaustive? It is true that, for Scholasticism, all human cognition

---

4. Karl Werner, *Franz Suarez und die Scholastik der letzten Jahrhunderte* ("Francisco Suarez and the Scholasticism of the last centuries"), p. 122.

coincides essentially with this form of cognition. Another writer who is very familiar with Scholasticism characterizes the concept of cognition of that philosophy this way:

> Our spirit, in that it is associated with the body in earthly life, is primarily directed toward the surrounding world of matter. But it focuses on spirit in the world—that is, the essences, natures, and forms of things, the elements of existence that are akin to it and provide it with the rungs by which it ascends to the suprasensory. The field of our cognition is the realm of experience, but we should learn to understand what it offers, penetrate to its sense and idea, and thereby open to ourselves the world of ideas.[5]

Scholastics could not attain a different concept of cognition. They were prevented from doing so by the dogmatic teaching of their theology. If they had fixed their spiritual gaze upon what to them was a mere image, they would have observed that the spiritual meaning of things reveals itself in this so-called image. They would then have found that God is not merely *mirrored* within human beings but that he *lives in them*. He is present in the human essence. In looking within, they would not have stared at a dark abyss of endless emptiness or at a mere image of God; instead, they would have felt that divine life itself vibrates within the human being and that their own lives are one with the life of God. Scholastics could not acknowledge this. In their opinion, God could not enter the human being and speak from an individual; he could exist there only as an image.

In reality, it had to be assumed that Divinity exists outside the self. God must *reveal* himself through *supranatural* communications from outside and cannot do so within, through the spiritual life. It is precisely this kind of thinking that is least likely to achieve the intended result—that is, the most sublime concept of Divinity.

---

5. Otto Willmann, *Geschichte des Idealismus* ("History of Idealism"), v. 2, 2nd ed., p. 396.

But this kind of thinking reduces Divinity to a thing among other things. Aspects of the world reveal themselves to the human being through experience, while God is thought to reveal himself in a supranatural way. One proposes a difference between the perception of Divinity and of creation in saying that, with respect to creation, external reality is given in the experience, that one has *knowledge* of it.

The experience of Divinity does not produce an object; one can attain this only through *faith*. To Scholastics the highest ideas are not objects of knowledge; they are objects of faith alone. It is true that according to the Scholastic view, the relationship of knowledge to faith is not to be imagined in such a way that, in a certain field, *only* knowledge predominates, and in another *only* faith:

> Cognition of what exists is possible for us, because it originates in a creative insight. Things are *for* spirit because they are *from* spirit; they tell us something because they receive their meaning from a higher intelligence.[6]

Since God has created the world according to his ideas, when we grasp the ideas of the world, we can also grasp the traces of Divinity in the world through scientific reflection. But we can know the nature of God in his essence only through supranatural revelation, which requires our belief. Our thoughts about the highest ideas are not decided by any human knowledge but by faith, and "to faith belongs everything contained in the Scriptures of the New and Old Covenant, and in the divine traditions."[7] We cannot assume the task here of a detailed description and an explanation of the relationship between the meaning of faith and that of knowledge.

Indeed, the essence of all faith originates in inner, human experience. It is preserved, according to its external worth, with no consciousness of how it was acquired. It is said that it came into the

---

6. O. Willmann, *Geschichte des Idealismus* ("History of Idealism"), v. a, p. 383.
7. Joseph Kleutgen, *Die Theologie der Forfeit* ("The Theology of Antiquity"), v. 1, p. 39.

world through supranatural revelation. The essence of the Christian faith was simply accepted as tradition by the Scholastics. Science and inner experience were not allowed to claim any rights over it. Scholastics could no more permit themselves to create a concept of God than scientists can create a tree; they had to accept the revealed concept as given, just as natural scientists accept the tree as given. Scholastics could never admit that spirit itself shines and lives within human beings. Consequently, they established a boundary for the jurisdiction of science at the point where the area of outer experience ends. Human cognition could not be permitted to produce a concept of the higher entities. Human beings were to accept a revealed one. The Scholastics could not concede that, by accepting this concept, they in fact embraced an idea that had been produced at an earlier stage of human spiritual life and declared to be a revelation.

In the course of the development of Scholasticism, all those ideas disappeared from it that still indicated the way human beings arrive at concepts of Divinity in a natural way. During the first centuries of the development of Christianity, at the time of the church fathers, we see how the teachings of theology came into being little by little through the inclusion of inner experiences. This is still treated entirely as an inner experience by John Scotus Eriugena, who stood at the height of Christian theological learning in the ninth century.[8] Among the Scholastics of the succeeding centuries, this quality of an inner experience is completely lost; the old meaning is reinterpreted as an external, supranatural revelation. One can interpret the activity of the mystical theologians Eckhart, Tauler, Suso, and their companions by saying that they were inspired by the teachings of the

---

8. John Scotus Eriugena (c.810–c.877), theologian and philosopher from Ireland, was invited to teach at the court of Charles II near Laon and to assist Hincmar of Reims in the controversy over predestination. Later he was condemned by the council of Valencia (855). He translated into Latin and commented on the works of Pseudo-Dionysius the Areopagite, St. Maximus the Confessor, St. Gregory of Nyssa, and St. Epiphanius. He tried to reconcile neo-Platonist emanationism and Christian creationism. Pope Honorius II condemned his work (1225) as pantheistic.

church (as contained in theology but reinterpreted) to reproduce a similar meaning from themselves as an inner experience.

Nicholas of Cusa began the task of ascending independently to inner experiences from the knowledge one acquires in the various sciences. There can be no doubt that the excellent technique of logic that the Scholastics had developed (and in which Nicholas had been educated) furnished a superb means of attaining inner experiences, even though the Scholastics themselves were kept from this road by their positive faith. But one will fully understand Nicholas only by realizing that his vocation as priest, which raised him to the position of cardinal, prevented him from breaking completely with the faith of the church, whose contemporary expression was found in Scholastic theology. We find him so far advanced along a certain path that every step would have led him, of necessity, out of the church. Consequently, we understand the cardinal best if we complete that step that he did not take and then, in retrospect, illuminate what had been his intention.

The most important concept of the spiritual life of Nicholas is that of "learned ignorance." By "learned ignorance," he means a higher form of cognition than is represented by ordinary knowledge. Knowledge in the lower sense means that spirit comprehends an object. The most important characteristic of knowledge is that it gives information about an entity outside spirit—that is, knowledge looks at something that spirit itself is not. In knowledge, the spirit is occupied with matters considered to be outside it. But what the spirit forms in itself concerning objects of the outer world is their *essence*. Things *are* spirit. At first, the human being sees the spirit only through the sensory covering. What remains outside the spirit is only this sensory covering; the essence of things enters into the spirit.

When spirit views this essence—which is substance of its substance—it can no longer speak of knowledge. It does not observe an object outside; it looks upon a thing that is part of itself. It looks at itself. It no longer knows; it only observes itself. It is not concerned with "knowing" but with "*not knowing*." It no longer takes hold of the world through spirit; it "beholds, without grasping," its own life. The highest level of cognition, in relation to the lower levels, is "not knowing." The essence of things can be communicated only at this level of perception.

With his "learned not knowing," Nicholas of Cusa speaks only of knowledge reborn as inner experience. He himself tells how he came to have this inner experience:

> I made many attempts to unite my thoughts about God and the world, about Christ and the church, in one fundamental idea. But none satisfied me until finally, during my return from Greece by sea, the gaze of my spirit lifted, as if through an inspiration from on high, to the view in which God appeared to me as the highest unity of all contrasts.[9]

Nicholas's predecessors more or less played a role in this inspiration. In his mode of thinking, we recognize a peculiar renewal of the ideas encountered in the writings of a certain Dionysius. John Scotus Eriugena (mentioned earlier) translated that work into Latin. He called the author the "great and divine revealer."[10] These writings first came to light in the first half of the sixth century. They were ascribed to Dionysius the Areopagite, who is mentioned in the Acts of the Apostles and was converted to Christianity by Paul. We shall not go into the question of when these writings were really composed. Their essence had a strong effect on Nicholas, as they had on John Scotus Eriugena. In many respects, they also stimulated the way of thinking of Eckhart and his companions. The "learned not knowing" is prefigured in a certain way in these writings. Here we shall record only the main characteristic of the thinking inherent in these writings.

---

9. Letter from the author to Cardinal Julianus, at the end of *De docta ignorantia*, vol. 3.
10. Dionysius the Areopagite (c. A.D. 500), an author whose identity is considered a mystery. He is thought to have originated in Syria and has been considered to be a convert of St. Paul. His primary works are *The Celestial Hierarchy* and *The Divine Names*.

People learn first about the things of the sensory realm. They reflect on the existence and activity of this world. The primordial foundation of all things must exist in a higher realm than the things themselves. People therefore cannot expect to comprehend that primordial foundation with the same concepts and ideas with which they grasp the things themselves. If people attribute to the primordial foundation (God) qualities they are familiar with from the lower realm, such qualities can be merely auxiliary ideas of the weak spirit, which draws the primordial foundation down to itself so that people can imagine it. In fact, no quality that lower phenomena possess can be said to belong to God. It cannot even be said that God exists. "Being," too, is a concept that human beings have formed in connection with lower phenomena, but God is exalted above "being" and "not being."

Consequently, the god to whom we ascribe qualities is not the true one. We arrive at the true god if we imagine a "Supra-God" above a god with those qualities. We can know nothing of this "Supra-God" in the ordinary sense. To reach such a god, "knowing" must flow into "unknowing." One can see that such a view is based on the awareness that human beings themselves can, in a purely natural way, develop a higher form of cognition from the knowledge provided by the sciences. This perception is no longer mere knowledge. The Scholastic view declared that knowledge lacks the capacity for such development, and at the point where knowledge is supposed to end, it claimed faith, based on external revelation as the aid of knowledge. Nicholas of Cusa was on the way toward once again developing knowledge in a way that the Scholastics had declared impossible.

From the point of view of Nicholas of Cusa, one cannot say that there is only one kind of knowing. On the contrary, cognition is clearly divided into the medium for knowing external reality and the object itself of such knowledge. The former kind of apprehension predominates in the sciences as the knowledge we acquire about the objects and processes of the sensory world. This kind of perception is active when we ourselves *live* in the knowledge that has been acquired. The second kind of comprehension develops from the first. Yet it is the same world to which both kinds of cognition refer, and it is the same human being who partakes of both. The question must follow, How does it happen that one and the same person develops two kinds of perception of one and the same world? The direction in which we must search for the answer was indicated in our discussion of Tauler. This answer can be even further defined with regard to Nicholas of Cusa.

First, the human being lives as a separate (individual) being among other separate beings. In addition to the influences that other beings exercise upon one another, the faculty of (lower) cognition is found in the individual human being. Through the senses, we receive impressions of other beings and work on those impressions with our spiritual faculties. We direct our spiritual gaze away from external things and look at ourselves, at our own activity. In this way, self-knowledge arises within us. As long as we remain at this level of self-knowledge, we do not yet see ourselves in the true sense of the word. We can maintain the belief that there is some hidden entity at work within us and that what appears to us as our own activity is merely the manifestation and action of the other entity.

The moment may come when people understand—through an indisputable inner experience—that what they perceive and encounter within themselves is not the manifestation or activity of a hidden force or entity but, instead, that entity itself in its primordial form. Such a person may then say, "All other things I encounter as given, in a sense, and I, standing outside them, add to them what spirit has to say about them. But I live through creatively adding to things in myself, and I discover what I am. I find my own essence."

What is speaking in the depths of my spirit? It is knowledge that speaks, the knowledge I have acquired about the things of the world. It is not an action or manifestation that speaks. The source of that speaking holds back none of its essence. In *this* knowledge the world speaks in all its immediacy. But I have acquired this knowledge from phenomena and from myself, as a being among other beings. Out of my own essence, I myself and world phenomena speak. I no longer express merely my own nature; I express the nature of things. My I-being is the form, the means, through which things declare themselves. I have come to know that I experience my own essence within myself; for me, this experience becomes enlarged into another. In me and through me, universal essence expresses itself or, in other words, knows itself. Now I can no longer feel that I am merely a thing among things; I can sense that I am a form in which universal essence has its life. Consequently, it is only natural that one and the same person should have two kinds of cognition.

With regard to sensory facts, the human being is of the world. Insofar as this is the case, people come to know things of the world, but at any moment they can have the higher experience that they are the form in which universal essence sees itself. Then they themselves are transformed from an entity among other entities into a form of the universal essence—and with them the knowledge of things is changed into an expression of the nature of things. This transformation, however, can be accomplished only by human beings themselves. The object of higher cognition is not present until higher perception itself is present. Only by manifesting a more advanced awareness can human beings develop their nature, and only through higher cognition can the nature of phenomena come into existence.

If people are not allowed to add anything to sensory perception through higher cognition but express only what exists as given by the outside world, this really means renouncing all higher cognition. With regard to sensory life, human beings are entities among other entities and attain higher cognition only when, as sensory beings, they transform themselves into higher beings. It follows that they can never replace one cognition with the other. Rather, spiritual life is made up of a perpetual, back-and-forth movement between two poles of cognition, between *knowing* and *seeing*. If people were to shut themselves off from seeing, they would forgo the nature of things. If they were to shut themselves off from sensory knowing, they would deprive themselves of the things whose nature they want to understand. The same things reveal themselves to the lower understanding and to the higher seeing, but at one time in terms of external appearance and another time with regard to inner essence. It is not inherent to the nature of things that they appear only as external objects at a certain stage. Rather, this happens because people must first transform themselves to the point where the things of the world cease to have only an external reality.

It is only with these considerations in mind that certain views elaborated by natural science during the nineteenth century appear in their proper light. Adherents of those views would say, "We hear, see, and touch the things of the material world through the senses. The eye, for example, communicates a light phenomenon—a color. We say that a body gives off *red* light when, through the medium of our eyes, we experience the sensation "red." But in other cases, the eye gives us another sensation. If the eye is struck or pressed or if an electric current passes through the head, the eye experiences a sensation of light. When we have the sensation that a body gives off a certain color of light, something may be happening in that body that does not in any way resemble color. Regardless of what is occurring in the outer world, as long as the process can make an impression upon the eye, a sensation of color arises. Our perception arises in us, because our organs are constituted in a certain way. Occurrences in the outer world remain outside us; we know only the *effects* that external processes produce within us.

Hermann Helmholtz (1821–1894) expressed this idea in a clearly defined way.

> Our perceptions are effects produced in our organs by external causes. The way those effects manifest depends substantially on the kind of apparatus they work on. Insofar as the quality of our perception provides information that characterizes the external influence that created it, one may consider it to be an *indication* of the influence but not a *representation* of it. We require an

image to be somewhat similar to the object represented. We likewise require similarity of form in a statue; a similarity of perspective in the field of view of a drawing; and, in addition to the perspective, a similarity of colors in a painting. But a sign needs no resemblance to the external object. The relationship between the two is limited: the same object, given the same circumstances, must evoke the same sign. Accordingly, unlike signs always correspond to unlike influences.... If, in the course of ripening, berries of a certain variety develop both a red pigment and sugar, then red color and sweet taste will always be found together in our perception of berries of this kind.[11]

I have described in detail this kind of thinking in *Intuitive Thinking as a Spiritual Path: A Philosophy of Freedom* and in *Riddles of Philosophy*.

Now, let us follow step by step the train of thought adopted by this view. A process is assumed to occur in the outer world. It produces an effect on my sensory organ; my nervous system transmits the resulting impression to my brain, and another process is produced there. I now perceive "red." It is said that, therefore, the perception of the color red is not outside me but within me. All our perceptions are only signs of external processes, the true nature of which we know nothing. We live and act among our perceptions and know nothing of their origin. In line with this way of thinking, we can also say that, if we had no eyes, there would be no color. Nothing would then transform the external process, which is unknown to us, into the perception "red."

This train of thought is seductive to many people. Nevertheless, it is based on a complete misinterpretation of the facts under consideration. (If many contemporary natural scientists and philosophers were not seriously deluded by this way of thinking, we would

---

11. Hermann Helmholtz, *Die Tatsachen der Wahrnehmung* ("The Facts of Perception"), pp. 12ff.

not need to speak about it so much. But this delusion has, in fact, corrupted contemporary thinking in many ways.) Because we are entities among other entities, the things of the world must make an impression upon us if we are to discover anything about them. A process outside the human being must give lead to a process within us if red is to appear in the field of our vision. One must only ask, What is outside, and what is inside? Outside is a process in space and time. But inside there is certainly a similar process. Such a process exists in the eye and communicates itself to the brain when I perceive red. I cannot directly observe the process that takes place inside any more than I can directly perceive in the outer world the motion of light waves, which physicists believe corresponds to the color red. It is only in this sense, however, that I can speak of outer and inner qualities. Only in terms of *sensory perception* does the differentiation between outside and inside have any validity.

This perception leads me to assume a process of space-time in the outer world, though I cannot perceive it directly. Moreover, that same perception leads me to assume such a process exists within me, which I am also unable to perceive directly. But I also assume other spatio-temporal processes in ordinary life, which I cannot perceive directly. For example, I hear a piano played in the next room and assume that a human being having spatial dimensions sits at the piano and plays. My way of representing matters to myself is the same, whether I speak of processes *within* me or *outside* me. I assume that the characteristics of such processes are analogous to qualities of those processes perceived by my senses, but that, for certain reasons, they are inaccessible to my direct observation.

If I were deny that these processes involve all the qualities my senses reveal to me in the realm of space and time, it would be like the proverbial knife without a handle whose blade is missing. I can say only that spatio-temporal processes take place in the outer world and that they give rise to spatio-temporal processes within. Both are necessary if red is to appear in my field of vision. Insofar as it is not spatio-temporal, it would be useless to look for this red, whether outside or inside. If natural scientists and philosophers cannot find red in the outer world, neither should they attempt to look for it within. It is not inside in the same sense that it is not outside. To say that everything the sensory world presents to us is really an inner world of perceptions, and to look for something external that corresponds to it, is an impossible concept. Consequently, we cannot say that red, sweet, hot, and so on are *indications*, to which something very different in the outer world corresponds, and that, as such, they arise only within us. In fact, the effect produced within us as the result of an external process is quite different from what appears in the field of our perception.

If we want to refer to what arises in us as "signs," we can say that those signs appear within our organism as a way to communicate perceptions that, in their immediacy, are neither inside nor outside us. Rather they belong to that common world of which my external world and my interior world are only parts. It is true that, if I wish to grasp that common realm, I must rise to the higher level of cognition that recognizes neither inside nor outside.

(I am well aware that those who rely on the truism that our entire world of experience is made up of sensations of unknown origin will look down their noses at this exposition. Their view of it will be somewhat like that of Dr. Erich Adikes, who, in his work *Kant contra Haeckel* (Berlin, 1901), says condescendingly: "For the time being, people like Haeckel and thousands of his kind philosophize merrily away, completely unconcerned with theories of cognition or with critical introspection" (p. 120).[12] Such gentlemen have no idea of the insignificance of their own theories of cognition. They suspect a lack of critical introspection only in others. We shall not begrudge them their "wisdom."

Nicholas of Cusa has excellent ideas on exactly the point we are considering. He maintains a clear separation between the lower and higher forms of cognition. Consequently, on the one hand, he can

---

12. Ernst Haeckel (1834–1919), German philosopher and biologist. He was the first German to advocate Darwin's theory of evolution; he formulated the familiar biological dictum "ontogeny recapitulates phylogeny."

gain extensive insight into the fact that people, as sensory beings, experience within themselves only those processes that, as effects, must be *unlike* the corresponding external processes. On the other hand, the differentiation of types of cognition keeps him from confusing those inner processes with the realities that appear in our field of perception and that, in their immediacy, are neither outside nor inside but are elevated above such disparity.

Nicholas was "prevented by his priestly cloth" from following without reservations the path that this insight indicated to him.[13] We see him making a good beginning with the advance from "knowing" to "not knowing," but, at the same time, we must note that in the field of "not knowing" he has nothing to impart except the theological teachings offered to us by Scholasticism.

It is true that he knows how to develop this theology in an ingenious way. His teachings on providence, Christ, the Creation, the Redemption, and the moral life are completely in harmony with Christian dogma. In keeping with his spiritual direction, he might have said, "I am confident that human nature, having immersed itself in every science, can transform from within itself 'knowing' into 'unknowing,' and that, consequently, the highest cognition brings satisfaction." In this case, he would have rejected (which he did not) the traditional ideas of soul, immortality, Redemption, God, Creation, the Trinity, and so on, and would have upheld those that he himself had discovered.

Nicholas, however, was so immersed in Christian concepts that he could easily believe he was awakening his own proper, inner "unknowing," whereas he was, in fact, merely presenting the traditional views of his education. We must remember that he was standing before a fateful abyss in human spiritual life. He was a man of *science*, which initially removes people from their innocent concord with the world, which exists as long as they conduct their lives in a purely naïve way. While living such a life, people have a

---

13. Quoted from Giodano Bruno, *Gesammelte Werke* (Jena, 1909).

dim sense of their connection to the universe as a whole. They, like other beings, are integrated into the chain of natural effects. With knowledge, they separate themselves from the whole, thus creating a spiritual world within. Within this world, people confront nature in solitude. They have become richer, but this wealth is a difficult burden, initially weighing on each individual alone. People must find the way back to nature through their own resources. They must understand that now they themselves must integrate their wealth into the chain of universal effects, just as nature integrated their poverty previously. It is here that all the evil demons lie in wait for human beings, whose strength can easily fail. Instead of accomplishing that integration themselves, people take refuge in revelation from outside, which delivers them from solitude and directs the knowledge they experience as a burden back to the primordial origin of existence, Divinity. They will think, as did Nicholas of Cusa, that they are walking their own road, while in reality they find only the road their spiritual development has shown them.

In general, there are three paths upon which one can walk once one arrives at the point Nicholas had reached. One is *positive faith*, which comes to us from outside. The second is *despair*, when one stands alone with one's burden and feels all existence shattered with oneself. The third path is the *self-development* of one's deepest faculties. One necessary quality that leads one along this third path is *confidence* in the world, and the other is the *courage* to follow that confidence no matter where it leads.

Addendum (1923): In a few words I hint here at the path to the cognition of spirit I described in my later writings, especially in *How to Know Higher Worlds*, *An Outline of Esoteric Science*, and *Riddles of the Soul*.

Agrippa of Nettesheim & Theophrastus Paracelsus

HEINRICH CORNELIUS AGRIPPA of Nettesheim and Theophrastus Paracelsus followed the path indicated by the thought of Nicholas of Cusa.[1] They immersed themselves in nature and, as comprehensively as possible, endeavored to explore its laws with all the means available at the time. In this knowledge of nature they also saw the true foundation for all higher cognition. They themselves tried to develop that foundation from natural science by allowing science to be reborn in the spirit.

---

1. Heinrich Cornelius Agrippa of Nettesheim (1486–1535), German physician, theologian, and philosopher; after serving in the army of Emperor Maximilian I he became a lecturer and historiographer to Emperor Charles V; he published *De occulta philosophia* (1531), a cosmology based on cabalistic and Pythagorean analyses and magic, which helped link his name to the legend of Faust; he rejected all scientific knowledge in favor of simple biblical piety.

Theophrastus Paracelsus (Bombast von Hohenheim, 1493–1541), German alchemist and physician born in Einsiedeln, Switzerland; he investigated the mechanics of mining, minerals, and diseases of miners in the mines of Tirol; he wandered Europe, Russia, and the Middle East; he was forced from the University of Basel for his defiance of tradition, choosing to lecture in German, and criticizing the classics; he opposed the humoral theory of disease, claiming instead that diseases are specific entities that can be cured by specific remedies; he emphasized the value of phenomenology, and was first to connect goiter with minerals in drinking water, describe silicosis, and identify congenital syphilis; he introduced therapeutic mineral baths of opium, mercury, lead, sulphur, and so on, thus establishing chemistry's place in medical practice.

Agrippa of Nettesheim led an eventful life. He was born in Cologne, the descendent of a noble family. He studied medicine and jurisprudence at an early age and informed himself about natural phenomena in the way that was customary of the time and within certain circles and societies, as well as through contact with several scholars who carefully kept secret whatever insights they gained into nature. To that end, he repeatedly went to Paris, Italy, and England, and he also visited the well-known Abbot Trithemius of Sponheim in Würzburg.[2] He taught in scientific institutions at various times, and here and there entered the services of rich and noble persons, at whose disposal he placed his talents as a statesman and scientist. His biographers describe the services he rendered as not always above reproach, and it is said that he acquired money under the pretext of being adept in secret arts and of securing various advantages for people by means of these arts. If this is true, it is balanced by his unmistakable and ceaseless urge to acquire the entire scope of learning of his time honestly and to deepen this knowledge in the spirit of a higher cognition of the world. He tried to gain a clear understanding of both natural science and higher cognition. Only one who has insight into the ways by which one achieves these two forms of cognition can attain such a goal.

It is true that natural science must be lifted into the realm of spirit before it can lead to higher cognition. Likewise, it is true that, initially, it must remain in its own proper field so that it may provide the right foundation for a higher level of understanding. "Spirit in nature" exists only for spirit. As surely as nature is spiritual in this sense, it is equally certain that nothing perceived in nature by physical organs is directly spiritual. Nothing that is spirit can appear to my eye as spirit. I must *not* seek spirit itself in nature. I do this when I interpret a process of the outer world in an directly spiritual way, as when, for example, I ascribe to plants a soul that is

---

2. Johannes Heidenberg (1462–1516), also known as Johannes Trithemius, a German abbot and historian. Abbot of Sponheim and of the Scottish monastery of St. Jakob in Würzburg.

only remotely analogous to the human soul. I also do this when I ascribe a spatial or temporal existence to spirit or to soul itself, when, for example, I say of the eternal human soul that it lives in time without the body but still in the manner of a body, rather than as pure spirit. And I do this even when I believe that the spirit of a deceased person can show itself in some sort of sensory perceptible manifestation.

Spiritualism commits this error and shows merely that it has not understood the true nature of spirit but simply wants to see spirit directly as a crude, sensory manifestation. It fails to understand the nature of the senses or spirit. To consider spirit directly as something rare, surprising, and unusual, spiritualism deprives spirit of ordinary sensory phenomena, which occurs hour after hour before our eyes. It fails to understand that, to someone with the capacity to see spirit, what lives as "spirit in nature" reveals itself, for example, in the collision of two elastic spheres. The revelation of this spirit is not limited to processes that are remarkable because of their unusual nature and the fact that they cannot be grasped directly in their natural context.

Furthermore, spiritualists draw the spirit down into a lower sphere. They do not explain a sensory perceptible phenomenon in space by means of those forces and beings that are, in turn, only spatial and available to the senses; rather, they resort to "spirits," which they then equate fully with what the senses perceive. This way of thinking is based on an insufficient capacity to comprehend spirit. One is incapable of viewing spirit in a spiritual way. Consequently, through mere sensory beings, one satisfies a need for spirit presence. To such people, spirit does not reveal spirit; this is why they look for it through the senses. They see clouds sailing through the air, and similarly they want to see spirits hurrying along.

Agrippa of Nettesheim fought for a truly natural science that does not attempt to explain natural phenomena through spiritual beings who haunt the world of the senses, but instead sees only what is natural in nature and only what is spiritual in spirit. Of course, it would be a complete misunderstanding of Agrippa to compare his natural science with that of later centuries, which has at its disposal completely different known facts. In such a comparison it might easily seem that he still attributes the effects of natural causes, or ideas based on erroneous information, to the direct action of spirits. Moritz Carriere does him this injustice when he says (though not with ill will):

> Agrippa gives a long list of the things that belong to the Sun, the Moon, the planets, or the fixed stars, and receive their influences. For instance, related to the Sun are fire, blood, laurel, gold, topaz; they bestow the gift of the Sun's courage, serenity, and light.... The animals have a sense of nature that, more exalted than human reason, approaches the spirit of prophecy.... People can be made to love and hate, to become sick and healthy. Thus one casts a spell upon thieves that prohibits them from stealing, prohibits merchants from trading, prohibits ships and mills from motion, and prevents lightning from striking. This is done with potions, salves, images, rings, and charms; the blood of hyenas or dragons is suitable for this purpose. One is reminded of Shakespeare's cauldron of the witches.[3]

One is *not* reminded of it, if one understands Agrippa correctly. He did, of course, believe ideas that were thought to be incontrovertible during his time. But we also do this today with regard to what is considered "factual." Are we to believe that future centuries will not cast much of what we have established as irrefutable facts into the closet of "blind" superstition? It is true that I am convinced that there is real progress in human knowledge. Once the "fact" that the Earth is round had been discovered, all earlier suppositions were banished into the realm of "superstition." So it is with certain

---

3. Moriz Carrière (1817–1895), French philosopher and aesthete; *Die philosophische Weltanschauung der Reformationszeit in ihren Beziehungen zur Gegenwart* (Leipzig, 1887), pp. 107ff.

truths of astronomy, biology, and so on. The doctrine of natural descent, in comparison with all earlier hypotheses of creation, represents progress that is similar to the idea of a round Earth compared to previous assumptions about its shape.

Nevertheless, I am aware that, in our learned scientific works and treatises, there are many so-called facts that will not appear as facts to future centuries any more than much of what was maintained by Agrippa and Paracelsus does today. It is not a question of what they considered to be facts but of the spirit in which they interpreted those facts. In Agrippa's time one found little comprehension of the "natural magic" that he advocated, which seeks what is natural in nature and only what is spiritual in spirit. People held on to the "supernatural magic" that seeks spirit in the realm of the senses, which Agrippa fought against. This is why Abbot Trithemius of Sponheim advised him to communicate his views as a secret doctrine only to a chosen few, who were able to rise to a similar view of nature and spirit; *we give oxen only hay, not sugar as we do to songbirds.*

It is perhaps this abbot to whom Agrippa owes the right viewpoint. In his *Steganographia*, Trithemius treats (with veiled irony) the way of thinking that confuses nature with spirit. In this book he seems to speak entirely about supernatural phenomena. One who reads it as it is must conclude that the author is speaking of conjuring spirits, of their flight through the air, and so on. But if one omits certain words and letters in the text, there remain letters that, when assembled into words, describe purely natural phenomena (as Wolfgang Ernst Heidel showed in 1676).[4] (In one case, for example, in a formula of incantation, one must completely omit the

---

4. Wolfgang Ernst Heidel (n.d.), counselor to the Archbishop of Mainz, claimed to have decoded the "Third Book" of the trilogy. But Heidel caused dismay by encrypting his solution, causing many to dismiss his claim. "Ultimately, Trithemius' sleight of hand was effective. 'People believe what they read.'... If Trithemius said his technique relied on talismans and planetary spirits, that's what people believed." (see Byron Spice, "German Monk's 500-Year-Old Mystery Solved," *Pittsburgh Post-Gazette*, Monday, June 29, 1998).

first and the last words and then cross out every other word starting with the second. In the remaining words, one must cross out every other letter, starting with the first. One then assembles into words that which remains, and the formula of incantation is transformed into a communication of a purely natural meaning.)

How difficult it was for Agrippa to work his way out of the prejudices of his time and rise to a clear view is established by the fact that he did not allow his *De occulta philosophia* to be published until 1531.[5] He had composed it as early as 1510 but considered it immature. Further evidence of his reticence is provided by his work *De vanitate scientiarum*, in which he speaks bitterly of the scientific and general activity of his time.[6] There he says very clearly that he had liberated himself only with difficulty from the delusion of those who see direct spiritual processes in external events, prophetic hints about the future in outer facts, and so on.

Agrippa progresses to higher cognition in three stages. The first stage deals with the world as presented to the senses, with substances and with physical, chemical, and other forces. At this stage he terms nature *elemental*. The second stage sees the world as a whole in its natural relationships and arrangements of everything related to measurement, number, weight, harmony, and so on. The first stage brings together the attributes that are closely related and looks for the causes of a phenomenon in its immediate environment. The second stage looks at a single phenomenon in relation to the cosmic whole. Agrippa posits the idea that each thing is under the influence of all the remaining things of the cosmic whole. This universal whole appears as a great harmony, of which every individual entity is a part. Seen from this perspective, the world is designated by Agrippa as the astral, or celestial, world. The third stage of cognition is where spirit, through immersion in itself, looks

---

5. Henry Cornelius Agrippa, *Three Books of Occult Philosophy*, J. Freake (trans.), D. Tyson (ed.), St. Paul: Llewellyn Worldwide, 1993.
6. *Of the Vanitie and Uncertaintie of Artes and Sciences*, Northridge, CA: California State University, 1974.

directly at spirit, the primordial essence of the world. Here Agrippa speaks of the "spiritual soul" world.

The views developed by Agrippa about the world and the human relationship to it may be encountered in a similar form in Theophrastus Paracelsus, where they are more complete and thus better considered in that work.

Paracelsus characterized himself when he wrote under his portrait, "No one who can stand alone should be the servant of another." His whole position with regard to cognition is given in these words. He himself wanted to go back to the foundations of natural science in order to ascend, through his own powers, to the highest regions of cognition. As a physician, he did not want to simply accept, like his contemporaries, what the old investigators had affirmed in the past, though they were considered authorities at the time (Galen and Ibn Sina, for example).[7] Paracelsus wanted to read directly in the book of nature:

> Physicians must completely examine nature, which is the world and all its causation. And the lessons of nature must be committed to their wisdom, seeking nothing in their own wisdom but only in the light of nature.[8]

He did not retreat from anything in his efforts to know nature and its manifestations from every aspect. For this purpose he traveled to Sweden, Hungary, Spain, Portugal, and the East. He was able to say:

---

7. Claudius Galen (129–c.199), Greek physician to gladiators in Pergamum and to the court in Rome of Marcus Aurelius; considered founder of experimental physiology and demonstrated that arteries carry blood rather than air; Ibn Sina, also called Avicenna (980–1037), Islamic scientist and philosopher from Bukhara (in Uzbekistan); became court physician to Buyid prince Shams ad-Dawlah in Hamadan (in Iran); renown for his science and medical skills, he wrote numerous works on science, language, religion, and philosophy.

8. Franz Strunz, *Paracelsus Volumen Paramirum und Opus Paramirum* (Jena, 1904), vol. 1, p.85.

> I have pursued the art despite danger to my life, and I have not been ashamed to learn from passers-by, hangmen, and barbers. My teachings have bean tested more severely than silver through poverty, anxiety, wars, and perils.[9]

Knowledge passed down from old authorities held no value for him; he believed that he could gain the correct view only by experiencing for himself the ascent from natural science to the highest cognition. He boldly articulated his experience:

> One who wants to pursue the truth must come into my realm.... After me, not I after you, Ibn Sina, Rhases, Galen, Mesur! After me, and not I after you, you of Paris, you of Montpellier, you of Swabia, you of Meissen, you of Cologne, you of Vienna and whatever lies on the Danube and the river Rhine, you islands in the sea, you Italy, you Dalmatia, you Athens, you Greek, you Arab, you Israelite. After me, and not I after you! Mine is the realm![10]

It is easy to misinterpret Paracelsus because of his rough exterior, which sometimes hides his deep seriousness behind jest. He himself states:

> Nature has not made me subtle, nor have I been raised on figs and white bread but on cheese, milk, and oat bread. Therefore, I may well be uncivil to the excessively clean and overly refined; understanding is difficult between those brought up in soft clothes and those of us who were brought up among fir cones. I must seem rough, though to myself I appear gracious. How can I not be strange for one who has never gone wandering in the sun?[11]

---

9. P. R. Netzhammer, *Theophrastus Paracelsus: Das Wissenswerteste über dessen Leben, Lehre und Schriften* (Berlin, 1904), pp. 30, 80.
10. Franz Strunz, *Das Buch Paragranum* (Leipzig, 1903), pp. 83, 11.
11. P. R. Netzhammer, op. cit., p. 85.

Goethe has beautifully described the relationship between humankind and nature (in his book on Winkelmann):

> When healthy human nature acts holistically, when people have a sense of themselves in a world that is a great, beautiful, noble, and valuable whole, when harmonious ease affords them pure and free delight, then the universe, if it could experience itself, would exult, *as having attained its goal,* and *admire the climax of its own becoming and essence.*[12]

Paracelsus is deeply imbued with the sentiment expressed in such statements. From such sentiment the human mystery takes shape for him.

Now let us consider how this happens in Paracelsus's sense. Initially, the road that nature took to produce its highest achievement is hidden from human powers of comprehension. Nature has attained a climax, but this climax does not say, *I experience myself as the whole of nature,* but rather, *I feel like an individual human being.* What, in fact, is an act of the whole world that comprehends itself as a single, solitary being standing alone. Indeed, this is true human nature, that we must consider ourselves something other than what we are. And if this is a contradiction, then the human being can be called a contradiction come to life. In their own way, people are the world. They view their harmony with the world as a duality. They are the same as the world but repetitious, individuated beings. This view is the contrast that Paracelsus perceives as microcosm (human being) and macrocosm (universe). For him, the human being is the world writ small.

Spirit causes human beings to regard their relationship with the world in this way. Spirit seems bound to a single being, to one organism. In its whole nature, this organism belongs to the great chain of the universe. It is a link in the chain and exists only in relation to all

---

12. Franz Strunz, op. cit., vol. 2, p. 172.

other beings. Spirit, however, seems to be a result of a single organism. At first it sees itself as connected only with this organism. It tears the organism from the native soil from which it grew. According to Paracelsus, there is a deep connection between the human being and the entire universe that is hidden in the natural foundation of existence, a connection obscured by the presence of spirit. Spirit leads us to higher cognition by communicating knowledge to us and by bringing that knowledge to rebirth on a higher level. Its initial effect, however, is to mask for us our own connection with the universe.

Paracelsus saw that human nature initially falls into three classifications. The first is our sensory and corporeal nature—the organism that appears to us as a natural being among other natural beings, essentially no different than other natural beings. The second component is our hidden nature. This is a link in the chain of the whole world and is, consequently, not enclosed within our organism. Rather, influences are sent and received between it and the whole universe. The third division is the highest nature—our spirit. It lives only in a spiritual way. Paracelsus calls the first part of human nature the *elemental body;* the second he terms the ethereal, celestial or *astral body;* and the third part he calls *soul*. Paracelsus sees astral phenomena as an intermediate level, between purely corporeal phenomena and the true soul phenomena. Spirit conceals that natural foundation of our existence, but once it ceases its activity, such phenomena will become visible.

The simplest manifestation of this realm may be seen in the dream world. The images that flit through our dreams, with their peculiar and significant connections with the events in our environment and with our inner states, are produced by our natural foundation and obscured by the soul's brighter light. If a chair collapses near my bed, I may dream a whole drama, ending with the gunshot in a duel. Or my heart may begin to pound and I dream of a red-hot stove. Meaningful and significant natural manifestations appear to reveal a life that exists between purely organic functions and the thinking processes in spirit's bright consciousness. Related to this are all the phenomena of hypnotism and suggestion. In suggestion we can see the affect of one human being on another, which points to a relationship between natural beings that is obscured by the higher activity of spirit.

Thus it becomes possible to understand what Paracelsus describes as an astral body. It is the collection of natural influences to which we are exposed, or to which we can be exposed through special circumstances. These emanate from us without the involvement of our soul, nor may they be considered purely physical phenomena.

In this area, Paracelsus enumerates facts that we doubt today. But this is really unimportant when viewed from the perspective I have presented. Based on such views of human nature, Paracelsus divides human nature into seven aspects. They are the same as those we find in the teachings of the ancient Egyptians, the neo-Platonists, and the Cabala. Human beings are first of all physical, bodily beings. Consequently, we are subject to the same laws to which *any* body is subject. In this sense they are purely elemental bodies. Purely corporeal, physical laws combine in the process of organic life. Paracelsus designates the organic laws *Archaeus*, or *Spiritus vitae*—the organic raises itself to spirit-like manifestations that are not yet spirit. These are the astral manifestations. The functions of the animal spirit emerge from the astral processes.

People are sensory beings, combining their sensory impressions through reason. Thus the *intellectual (rational) soul* awakens in them. They immerse themselves in their own spiritual effects; they learn to recognize spirit as spirit. In this way, they raise themselves to the level of the *spiritual soul*. Finally, they understand that, in this spiritual soul, they experience the deepest stratum of universal existence; the spiritual soul is no longer individual and separate. This is the insight to which Eckhart referred when he felt that it was no longer he who spoke but primordial essence. Now a condition prevails in which universal spirit regards itself in the human being. Paracelsus expressed with simplicity the feeling aroused by this condition: "And this, which you must consider, is something great; there is nothing in Heaven nor on Earth that is not contained in the human being. And *God*, who is in Heaven, is in the human being."[13] It is only the facts of inner and outer experience that Paracelsus wants to express through the seven fundamental aspects of human nature.

For human experience, this plurality of seven parts is, in higher reality, a unity. Paracelsus does not question this. Higher cognition exists precisely to show the unity in everything that, to immediate experience, seems to us a plurality because of our bodily and spiritual organization. On the level of the highest knowing, Paracelsus strives to fuse the world's living, uniform, primordial essence with spirit. He knows, however, that people can know nature spiritually only when they enter immediate communion with it. People do not come to understand nature by populating it themselves with arbitrarily assumed spiritual entities but by accepting and valuing it as nature. Paracelsus, therefore, does not look for God or spirit in nature; for him nature, as it presents itself to his eye, is immediately *divine*.

Must one first attribute to the plant a soul like the human soul to find spirit? Paracelsus explains the development of phenomena (to the degree that this is possible with the scientific resources of his time) in such a way that he regards this development entirely a sensory process of nature. He lets everything arise from primordial matter, primordial water (*Yliaster*). And he regards as a further process of nature the separation of primordial matter (which he also calls the "great limbo") into the four elements of water, earth, fire, and air. When he says that "divine word" invoked the multiplicity of beings from primordial matter, this should be understood in somewhat the same way that contemporary natural science understands the relationship between force and matter. A "spirit" in the real sense is not yet present on this level. Spirit is not a cause of the natural process but a *result* of this process; it does not create nature but develops from it. Much of what Paracelsus says could be interpreted in the opposite sense. For example, he says:

---

13. Franz Strunz, *Paracelsus Volumen Paramirum und Opus Paramirum*, vol. 4, p. 279.

> There is nothing corporeal that does not carry a living spirit hidden within it. *All* corporeal and substantial things have life, not just those that stir and move, such as people and animals, the worms in the earth, the birds in the sky, and the fish in the water.[14]

Paracelsus uses such sayings only to warn against a superficial view of nature that believes one can exhaust the nature of a phenomenon with a few "forced" concepts (to use Goethe's apt expression). His intention is not to inject things with an invented quality but to promote the movement of our human faculties to produce the reality within a phenomenon. It is important not to be misled by the fact that Paracelsus expresses himself in the spirit of his time. Instead, one should try to understand what he has in mind when, viewing nature, he presents his ideas in the expressions of his time. For example, he ascribes to the human being a twofold flesh, that is, a twofold corporeal constitution.

> The flesh must be understood to be of two kinds—the flesh whose origin is in Adam and the flesh that is not from Adam. The flesh from Adam is coarse flesh, because it is earthly and only flesh, to be bound and grasped like wood and stone. The other flesh is not from Adam; it is subtle flesh, not to be bound or grasped, because it is not made of earth.[15]

What is the flesh that comes from Adam? It is all that has come down to the us through natural development, which we have thus inherited. Added to all this, in the course of time, all that we have acquired through interacting with our environment. Our contemporary scientific concepts of inherited characteristics and those acquired through adaptation arose from the thinking of Paracelsus.

---

14. Hans Kayser, *Vom Wesen der dinge: Schriften Theophrasts von Hohenheim genannt Paracelsus* (Leipzig, 1921), p. 299.
15. Jolan Jacobi, *Lebendiges Erbe* (Leipzig, 1942), p. 242.

The "subtler flesh," which makes the us capable of spiritual activities, has not been present in human beings from the beginning. They were of "coarse flesh" like the animals, a flesh that can be "bound and grasped like wood and stone." Consequently, in the scientific sense, the soul is also a characteristic acquired by this coarse flesh. When scientists of the nineteenth century speak of the inheritances from the animal world, they mean what Paracelsus meant by his expression, the "flesh that came from Adam."

These remarks, of course, are not intended to eliminate the difference between a natural scientist of the sixteenth century and those of the nineteenth century. After all, it was only in the nineteenth century that we gained the ability to see, in a fully scientific sense, the forms of living organisms so that their relationship in nature and true derivation in connections with the human being became evident. Science sees only a natural process, whereas Linnaeus, in the eighteenth century, still saw a spiritual process he characterized in this way: "There are as many species of living organisms as there were, in principle, forms that were *created*."[16] Whereas Linnaeus had to shift spirit into the spatial world and assign it the task of producing spiritually, or "creating" life forms, the natural scientist of the nineteenth century could attribute to nature what belongs to nature and to the spirit what belongs to spirit. Nature itself is given the task of explaining its creations, and the spirit can immerse itself in itself, where it alone may be found—within the human being.

In a certain sense, Paracelsus thinks very much in the spirit of his time; yet, it is exactly in terms of the idea of development, or becoming, that he profoundly comprehended the relationship between the human being and nature. He did not see existing, finished work in the world's primordial essence; he grasped instead the divinity in its becoming. Consequently, he could in truth ascribe self-creating

---

16. Carolus Linnaeus, *Genera plantarum* (Frankfurt, 1789), p. xii; Linnaeus, or Carl von Linné (1707–1778), Swedish botanist and founder of modern, systematic botany; became lecturer at Uppsala and explored Lapland. He was a medical doctor in Stockholm and a professor of medicine and botany, on which he wrote several works.

activity to the human being. If divine, primordial essence exists, once and for all a true creation by the human being is out of the question. Then it is not the human being, living in time, who creates, but God, who is eternal. For him there is only eternal becoming, and the human being is a link in this eternal becoming. Anything the human being forms did not exist previously in any way.

Whatever human beings create, as they create it, is an original creation. It can be called divine only in the sense that it exists as a human creation. Accordingly, in terms of cosmic creation, Paracelsus can assign a role to human beings that makes them co-architects in this creation. Divine, primordial essence is not the same without the human being. "Nature brings forth nothing into the light of day complete as it stands; rather, human beings must complete it."[17] The self-creating activity of the human being in the building of nature, Paracelsus calls *alchemy*. "This completion is alchemy. Alchemists are bakers when they bake bread, vintagers when they makes wine, weavers when they make the cloth."[18] Paracelsus wants to be an alchemist in his field, as a physician.

> I may fittingly write so much here about alchemy that you learn it well and know what it is and how it is to be understood and not be annoyed that it is not intended to bring you gold or silver. Rather see that the secrets are revealed to you.... The third pillar of medicine is alchemy, since remedies cannot be prepared without it, because nature cannot be put to use without art.[19]

Paracelsus's eyes are directed in the strictest sense at nature in order to discover from nature itself what it says about its products. He intends to investigate the laws of chemistry, so that he can work in this sense as an alchemist. He considers all bodies to be composed of three basic substances—salt, sulfur, and mercury. Paracelsus

---

17. Franz Strunz, *Das Buch Paragranum*, p. 70.
18. Ibid.
19. Ibid., pp. 86, 70.

identifies salt, sulfur, and mercury, of course, not as corresponding to the names used later by chemistry any more than he considers basic substance to be that of later chemistry. Various things are designated by the same names at different times. The ancients designated phenomena according to the four elements—earth, water, air, and fire—and these are still with us. We no longer call them "elements" but states of aggregation, which we term solid, liquid, gaseous, and ethereal. For example, for the ancients *earth* did not refer to the Earth but to "solidity." We can also recognize the three basic substances of Paracelsus in contemporary concepts, but not using similar, contemporary terms. Paracelsus uses the two important chemical processes of liquid solution and combustion. When a body is dissolved or burned, it is decomposed into its parts. A portion remains as residue, and another portion is dissolved or burned. He saw the residue as saline, the (liquid) soluble as mercurial, and the combustible as sulfurous.

Such natural processes may leave us cold if we fail to look beyond them, as we might by anything material and prosaic. Those who, at all costs, want to apprehend spirit through the senses will attribute all sorts of spiritual entities to those processes. Like Paracelsus, however, anyone who knows how to view such processes in relation to the universe (which reveals its secret within the human being), accepts those processes as they are presented to the senses. Such a person does not begin by reinterpreting them, because those natural processes as they confront us with their sensory reality reveal in their own way the mystery of existence. Those who struggle for the light of higher knowledge, through this sensory reality these processes reveal something out of the human soul that exists at a higher level—higher than all the paranormal wonders related to the so-called spirit that people devise or may have revealed to them. When the soul unites with that nature in friendship and, in intimate communication, heeds the revelations of its secrets, there is no "spirit of nature" that can express any higher truths than those revealed by the great works of nature themselves. Paracelsus sought that kind of friendship with nature.

Valentin Weigel &
Jacob Boehme

PARACELSUS WAS CONCERNED primarily with developing ideas about nature that breathe the spirit of the higher knowing he advocated. Valentin Weigel was a kindred thinker.[1] He applied the same kind of thinking to our own human nature. He developed out of Protestant theology, just as Eckhart, Tauler, and Suso developed from Catholic theology. His precursors were Sebastian Franck and Caspar Schwenckfeldt.[2] they emphasized the deepening of the inner life, in contrast to church dogma's attachment to an external creed. For them, it is not the Jesus about whom the Gospels preach who is of value, but rather the Christ who can be born in every human being out of one's deeper nature and who is to be the deliverer from the lower life and the leader in the ascent to the ideal. Weigel lived quietly and modestly as pastor of his church in Zschopau. It is only from his posthumous writings printed in the seventeenth century

---

1. See footnote on page 18.
2. Sebastian Franck (c.1499–c.1542), German theologian and originally a Catholic priest, he converted to the Reformed faith, but was accused of having Anabaptist tendencies. He came out against the emphasis on writing, and also against organization and external observances. He believed that each person has a divine element within, which is the source of spiritual life. He gloried in the heretics, and included in that group all who had gone a separate path in search of truth. Caspar Schwenckfeldt was a friend. He was a Hussite, and greatly supported the cause of Luther, but, because of disagreements with Luther over the subjects of baptism, the Lord's Supper, and justification, he left the Reformers. *(continued on following page)*

that one discovers the significant ideas he developed concerning human nature.[3]

Weigel was anxious to become clear about his relationship to the church's teachings and was consequently led to investigate the basis of cognition in general. People can decide whether they can know something through a creed only when they understand *how* they know. Weigel began with the most basic kind of cognition. He asked, How do I apprehend a sensory object that confronts me? From there he hoped to rise to the point where he could account for the highest form of cognition. In sensory apprehension the instrument (the sensory organ) and the object, the "counterpart," confront each other:

> In natural perception there must be two things—the object, or counterpart (which is to be perceived and seen by the eye) and the eye, or the perceiver, (which sees and perceives the object). Therefore, consider this question: Does perception arise from the object and flow into the eye, or does judgment, and perception, flow from the eye into the object?[4]

Weigel says that if perception flowed from the counterpart (the object) into the eye, then the same complete perception would have

---

2. *(continued from previous page)* He was strongly opposed to confining the Christian faith to precise dogmas and stressed instead the inner experience of God's grace. He became a wanderer, and those who followed him called themselves "Confessors of the Glory of Christ." Persecution eventually caused his followers to disperse. Caspar Schwenckfeldt von Ossig (1489–1561), German noble and mystic who experienced spiritual awakening in 1518 and became leader of the Protestant Reformation in Silesia; he disagreed with Luther's views on the Eucharist and founded the "Reformation by the Middle Way" movement, between Catholic and Lutheran theologies; eventually, he alienated so many that he became a religious fugitive about 1534; societies formed by his followers survive in the United States as the Schwenckfeldt church.

3. Three of Weigel's works: "The Golden art of Knowing Everything without Error, unknown to Many of the Learned, and yet Necessary for all Men to Know," "Know Thyself," and "Of the Place of the World."

4. *Der güldene Griff*, chap. 9

to arise in all eyes with respect to the same object. But this is not so; we all see according to our own eyes. Only the eyes, not the counterpart, can be responsible for the fact that many different views of one and the same thing are possible. In order to make the matter clear, Weigel compares seeing with reading. If the book did not exist, I could not read it. But it could be there, and I would still not be able to read anything in it if I did not know how to read. The book is there, but cannot itself give me anything; I must evoke within myself everything I read. This is also true of natural (sensory) perception. Color exists as a "counterpart" but, of itself, cannot offer anything to the eye. The eye itself must perceive color. The color is no more in the eye than the content of the book is in the reader. If the content of the book were in us as the readers, we would not have to read it. Nevertheless, in reading, this content does not flow out of the book but out of the readers. It is the same with sensory objects. The nature of the sensory object in its outer aspect does not flow into the human being from the outside but from the inside.

Based on these ideas, one could say that if all perception flows from the human being into the object, one does not perceive what is in the object but only what is within the person. The views of Immanuel Kant (1724–1804) present a detailed elaboration of this line of thinking.[5] Weigel says that, though perception flows from the human being, it is only the nature of the counterpart that emerges through the human observer. As it is the content of the book that I discover by reading, and not my own, so it is the color of the counterpart that I discover through the eye, not any color that is in the eye itself or in me. On his own path, Weigel thus concludes what we have already encountered in the thinking of Nicholas of Cusa.

---

5. I have shown the erroneous aspect of this train of thought in chapter 4 of *Intuitive Thinking As a Spiritual Path: A Philosophy of Freedom*. Here I must say only that, with this simple, straightforward way of thinking, Valentin Weigel stands on a much higher level than does Kant.—R. STEINER.

In his own way, Weigel elucidated the nature of sensory perception. He became convinced that whatever external objects can tell us can flow only from within us. We cannot remain passive when we want to perceive sensory objects; we cannot be content with allowing objects to act upon us but must become active and bring this perception out of ourselves. It is the counterpart that awakens perception in the spirit. The human being ascends to higher cognition when the spirit becomes its own object.

In considering sensory perception, one can see that no cognition can flow *into* the human being from the outside. Accordingly, higher cognition cannot arise outside but must be awakened within the human being. There can be no external revelation but only an inner awakening. The external object must wait until we confront it before it can express its nature; likewise, if we want to be our own counterpart, we must wait until perception of our nature is awakened within us. Whereas, in sensory perception we must become active to present the counterpart with its nature, in higher cognition we must remain passive, because we ourselves become the counterpart. We must awaken to our own inner nature. Consequently, spiritual knowledge appears as higher illumination.

Weigel therefore calls higher cognition, as opposed to sensory perception, the "light of grace." This light of grace is really nothing but the self-perception of human spirit—a rebirth of knowledge on a higher level of seeing. In pursuing his road from knowing to seeing, Nicholas of Cusa does not really allow the knowledge he acquires to be reborn on a higher level; rather, he is deceived into regarding the church creed, in which he had been educated, as this rebirth. This is the case with Weigel, too. He finds the right path and loses it again as soon as he begins it. If we want to follow the way indicated by Weigel, we can consider him the leader only up to the beginning of that path.

* * *

IN THE WORKS OF JACOB BOEHME, the master shoemaker of Görlitz, we encounter a kind of delight in nature that, at its peak, admires its essence.[6] Here is a man whose words have wings, woven from the blissful feeling that he sees his self-knowledge shining as higher wisdom. Boehme describes his condition as devotion that wants only to be wisdom; it is wisdom that desires only to live in devotion:

> When, with God's assistance, I wrestled and fought, a wondrous light arose within my soul that was completely foreign to wild nature. Through it I began to understand the nature God and human beings and the relationship of God to humankind.[7]

Boehme no longer experienced himself as a separate person declaring his insights. Rather, he saw himself as an agent of the great universal spirit speaking in him. To him, the limits of his personality did not seem to limit the spirit speaking from him; for him such spirit is omnipresent. He knows that the sophist will censure him whenever he speaks of the world's beginning and creation,

> because I was not there and did not see it myself. Let them be told that, when I was not yet the I but still Adam's essence, in the essence of my soul and body I was indeed there and that I have sacrificed my bliss in Adam.[8]

It is only in external similes that Boehme can suggest the nature of the light that shined within him. As a boy, he was once on the

---

6. Jacob Boehme (1575–1624), the German mystic, was influenced by the works of Paracelsus and other alchemists; he had a mystical experience in 1600; wrote *The Aurora* (1612), *The Three Principles of the Divine Essence* (1619), *The Way to Christ* (1624), and other works on esoteric Christianity; he was concerned in particular with the nature of evil and dualism; his work strongly influenced the development of idealism, Romanticism, and Quaker philosophy.
7. Jacob Boehme, *Apologia I contra Balthasar Tilken*, preface.
8. Jacob Boehme, *The Three Principles of the Divine Essence*, chapter 7.

summit of a mountain, above a spot where great, red stones seemed to enclose the mountain. He saw an entry in whose depths was a vessel of gold. He was overcome with awe and went on his way without touching the treasure. Later, when he was an apprentice with a shoemaker in Görlitz, a stranger walked into the store and asked for a pair of shoes. Boehme was not allowed to sell them to him in the master's absence. The stranger left, but after a while he called the apprentice outside and said, "Jacob, you are little, but one day you will become a completely different person who will astonish the whole world."

When he had become more mature, Jacob Boehme saw the Sun reflected in a burnished, pewter vessel; the sight that confronted him seemed to reveal a profound mystery. After his experience of that manifestation, he believed he possessed the key to the mysterious language of nature. He lived as a spiritual hermit and supported himself modestly by his trade. He wrote down, as if from memory, the notes that sounded within when he felt the spirit in him. The fanaticism of the priests made his life difficult. He wanted to read only the scripture that the light within illuminated for him, but he was pursued and tormented by those who had access only to the external scriptures of rigid, dogmatic creed.

Because a universal mystery lived in his soul, Jacob Boehme was filled with a restlessness that moved him toward knowledge. Within his spirit, he felt immersed in spiritual, divine harmony, but when he looked around, he saw disharmony everywhere in the divine works. The light of wisdom belongs to human beings who are nevertheless exposed to error. The impulse toward good lives in people, yet the dissonance of evil can be heard throughout the course of human evolution. Nature is governed by grand laws, yet its harmony is disturbed by excesses and the wild struggle of the elements.

How can we understand this disharmony in a harmonious, universal whole? This is the question that tormented Boehme. It came to the center of his world of ideas. He wanted to gain a concept of the universal whole that includes the disharmonious, because how is it possible to accept a worldview that omits and fails to explain the existing disharmony?

Disharmony must be explained through harmony, and evil through good. In discussing these matters, let us limit ourselves to good and evil. Disharmony in the narrower sense is expressed in human life. Basically, Boehme also limits himself to this concept. He can do this, because to him nature and the human being appear as essentially one; he sees laws and processes in both as similar. To him, everything in nature that does not serve a function is evil, just as evil is a nonfunctional element in human destiny. In both it is the same basic forces at work. To one those who understand the origin of evil in the human being, the origin of evil in nature is also obvious. How can it be that evil as well as good flow from the same primordial essence? In the spirit of Jacob Boehme, we must respond that the primordial essence does not exist only in itself. The world's diversity participates in this existence. The human body does not live its life as a single part but as a multiplicity; it is the same for primordial essence. Human life is poured into that multiplicity, and likewise the primordial essence is poured into the diversity of the world.

The human being as a whole has a *single* life, and each part likewise has a life of its own. And it would be just as contradictory for the whole harmony of human life for our hands to turn against our bodies and wound us than as it is for the things of the world—which, in their own way, live the life of the primordial essence—to turn against one another. Thus, in distributing itself over various lives, the primordial life bestows upon each life the capacity to turn against the whole. Evil does not flow from the good but from the way that good lives. Light can shine only when it penetrates the darkness, and the good can come to life only when it permeates its opposite. The abyss of darkness shines from the light; the good produces itself from the abyss of the indifferent. In a shadow, only brightness needs to be compared to light, whereas darkness is experienced as self-evident and something that weakens the light. Likewise, only the lawfulness of all things needs proof, whereas evil, or the nonfunctional, is accepted as self-evident. Although for Boehme the primordial essence is the all-in-all, nothing in the world can be understood unless we keep our eyes on both the primordial essence and its opposite.

> There is nothing in this world so evil that it does not contain good.... Every being has good and evil within itself, and in its development, having to decide between them, it becomes an opposition of qualities, since one of them seeks to overcome the other.[9]

Thus it is entirely in the spirit of Jacob Boehme to see both good and evil in the world's every object and process, but it is not in his spirit to seek the primordial essence without further ado in the mixture of good and evil. The primordial essence had to assimilate the evil, but the evil is not a part of the primordial essence. Boehme looked for the primordial foundation of the world, but the world itself arose from the abyss by way of the primordial foundation:

> The external world is not God and in eternity is not to be called God but is only a being in which God reveals himself.... It is correct to say that God is everything—that God is Heaven and Earth and also the outer world. Everything originates from him and in him. But what do I do with such a saying that is not a religion?[10]

With this view as a background, Boehme's ideas about the nature of the world developed in his spirit so that he saw the lawful world as arising out of the abyss in a succession of stages. This world is built up in seven natural forms. The primordial essence receives a dark, sour taste, silently enclosed within itself and motionless.

---

9. Jacob Boehme, *Mysterium magnum: An Exposition of the First Book of Moses Called Genesis*, chapter 10, number 15; and *177 Fragen von göttlicher Offenbarung* ("177 questions on divine revelation"), no. 2.
10. Jacob Boehme, *Anti-Stiefelius II*, 316; *Apologia II contra Balthasar Tilken*, 140.

Boehme uses salt to express this sourness symbolically. He uses such designations to lean on Paracelsus, who borrowed terms for natural processes from chemical processes. By incorporating its opposite, the first natural form assumes the shape of the second. The harsh and motionless incorporate motion—energy and life enter it. Mercury symbolizes the second natural form. In the struggle between stillness and motion, between death and life, the third natural form (sulfur) appears. This life, along with its inner conflict, is revealed to itself. After that, it no longer lives in the external struggle of its parts; like uniformly shining lightning illuminating itself, it delights in its own being (fire).

The fourth natural form then ascends to the fifth—the living struggle of the parts resting within itself (water). On this level there is an inner sourness and silence that is similar to the first. It is not an absolute quiet of inner contrasts, but an inner *movement* of contrasts. It is not quiet that rests within itself, but motion that was kindled by the fiery lightning of the fourth stage. On the sixth level, the primordial essence becomes self-aware in its inner life; it perceives itself through the sensory organs. Living organisms, endowed with senses, represent this natural form. Boehme calls it *sound*, or resonance, and thus establishes the sensory impression of hearing to symbolize sensory perception in general. The seventh natural form is the spirit elevating itself through its sensory perceptions (wisdom). It finds itself again as the primordial foundation within the world that has grown out of the abyss and formed itself from harmonious and inharmonious elements. "The Holy Spirit brings the splendor of majesty into the entity in which Divinity is revealed"[11]

Jacob Boehme attempted to use such ideas to fathom the world in keeping with the knowledge of his time. For him, the "facts" were established by the natural science of his time and by the Bible. His way of thinking is one thing and his world of facts another. One can imagine his way of thinking applied to a very different set

---

11. Jacob Boehme, *Vom dreifachen Leben des Menschen*, chapter 4, no. 82 and chapter 5, no. 39.

of facts. Accordingly, we see before us a Boehme who could be living at the beginning of the twentieth century. Such a man would not use his thinking to understand the biblical story of Creation and the struggle between the angels and devils; rather, he would use Lyell's *Principles of Geography* and Haeckel's *Natural History of Creation*.[12] One who gets through to an understanding of the *spirit of Boehme's writings must arrive at this conviction*.[13]

These words should not be understood to suggest that it would be an aberration in our time to investigate the Bible and the spiritual world. They simply mean that Jacob Boehme, if he were alive in the nineteenth century, would be led to a natural history of Creation by paths similar to those that led him to the Bible in the sixteenth century. But from there he would press toward the spiritual world.

---

12. Charles Lyell (1797–1875), English geographer. On Haeckel, see footnote, page 86.

13. We shall mention the most important of these writings: *The Coming of the Dawn; The Three Principles of the Divine Essence; On the Threefold Life of the Human Being; The Eye Turned Upon Itself; Signatura rerum or on the Birth and Designation of All Beings;* and *Mysterium magnum*.

Giordano Bruno & Angelus Silesius

AT CASTLE HEILSBERG in Prussia, during the first decade of the sixteenth century, the scientific genius Nicholas Copernicus erected a framework of ideas that compelled those of following eras to gaze at the starry heavens in a way unlike that of our predecessors of antiquity or the Middle Ages.[1] To the people of medieval times, the Earth was a dwelling at rest in the center of the universe. The stars, on the other hand, were perfect entities that moved in circles, the circle being the image of perfection. Human beings saw in the sensory manifestations of the stars something belonging directly to the soul or the spirit. The objects and events of the Earth spoke one language to humankind; while another language was spoken by the shining stars, which, in the pure ether beyond the Moon, seemed to be spiritual beings filling all of space. Nicholas of Cusa had formed different ideas. Through the explanations of Copernicus, the Earth became for humankind a fellow creation among heavenly bodies, a star that moved like any other. If anything on Earth

---

1. Nicholas Copernicus (Mikolaj Kopernik, 1473–1543), Polish astronomer and canon of Frauenburg cathedral; studied in Italy and became adviser and secretary to his uncle, bishop of Ermeland. He observed the orbits of Sun, Moon, and planets from 1497, and gradually abandoned the Ptolemaic system, positing instead his own heliocentric system in which Earth rotates daily on its axis and, along with other planets, revolves around the Sun; he published his revolutionary *De revolutionibus orbium coelestium* in 1543.

appeared somehow different, it could be attributed only to the fact that we live here. People were forced to stop viewing earthly phenomena any differently than they did phenomena in the rest of the universe. The sensory world had expanded into the most distant space. They had to accept that everything that reaches the eye from the ether is a part of the sensory realm, no different than the things of Earth. With the senses, they could no longer look for spirit in the ether.

After that, all who worked for higher knowledge had to come to terms with this expanded sensory world. In earlier centuries, the meditating human spirit had faced a different world. Now it was given a new task; it was no longer only the things of the Earth that could express their nature from the inner human being. This interior had to embrace the spirit of a sensory world—one that fills the spatial universe everywhere in the same way. This was the kind of task that confronted Giordano Bruno, the thinker from Nola.[2]

The senses had conquered the spatial universe for themselves; spirit could no longer be found in space. Consequently, human beings were prompted externally to look for spirit—on the basis of deep inner experiences—only where it had been sought by the

---

2. Filippo Bruno (1548–1600) was born in Nola, near Naples, the son of Giovanni Bruno, a soldier, and Fraulissa Savolino. He took the name Giordano upon entering the Dominican order. In the monastery in Naples where Thomas Aquinas had taught, Bruno studied Aristotelian philosophy. His exceptional abilities took him to Rome and to the Pope. During this period he may also have come under the influence of Giovanni Battista Della Porta, a Neapolitan polymath who published an important book on natural magic. Bruno was attracted to new streams of thought, among which were the works of Plato and Hermes Trismegistus, both resurrected in Florence by Marsilio Ficino in the late fifteenth century. Because of his heterodox tendencies, Bruno drew the attention of the Inquisition. For the next seven years he lived in France, lecturing on various subjects and published *Cena de le Ceneri* ("The Ash Wednesday supper") and *De l'Infinito, Universo e Mondi* ("On the infinite universe and worlds"), both in 1584. In *Cena de le Ceneri*, Bruno defended the heliocentric theory of Copernicus. In Venice he was arrested by the Inquisition and tried. After he had recanted, Bruno was sent to Rome in 1592 for another trial. For eight years he was kept imprisoned and interrogated. In the end, he refused to recant, was declared a heretic, and burned at the stake.

brilliant thinkers I have discussed in the preceding chapters. These thinkers drew out of themselves a worldview that a more advanced natural science would later force on humankind. The sun of ideas that later illuminated a new understanding of nature was still beyond the horizon for those thinkers, but even then its light appeared as a dawn when human thinking about nature was still enclosed within the darkness of night.

For the purposes of science, the sixteenth century gave the heavens to the world of the senses—to which they rightfully belong. Until the end of the nineteenth century, science had progressed to the degree that it could attribute to the sensory world what rightfully belonged to it among the phenomena of plant, animal, and human life. Science henceforth could look only for factual, sensory processes, whether in the ether or in the development of living organisms. The sixteenth-century thinker was compelled to say that the Earth is a star among stars, subject to the same laws as other stars. And the nineteenth-century thinker had to say,

> Whatever their origin and future may be, in the context of anthropology human beings are only mammals. Specifically they are mammals whose organization, needs, and diseases are the most complicated and whose brain, with its wonderful capacity, has reached the highest degree of development.[3]

Based on this view attained by science, the confusion about spirit and the sensory world became impossible if people understood themselves correctly. Advanced science makes it impossible to look in nature for a spirit conceived in a materialistic way, just as sound thinking compels us to look at the laws of mechanics to find out why the hands of a clock advance (the spirit of inorganic nature), rather than looking for a particular demon who causes the

---

3. Paul Topinard, *Anthropologie*, (Anthropology, Leipzig, 1888), p. 528.

hands to move. As a scientist, Ernst Haeckel justifiably rejected the clumsy view of a material god:

> In the higher, more abstract forms of religion, this corporeal manifestation is abandoned, and God is worshipped only as *pure spirit*, without body. "God is a Spirit: and they that worship him must worship him in spirit and in truth" [John 4:24]. Nevertheless, the spiritual activity of this pure spirit is exactly the same as that of the anthropomorphous, divine personality. In reality, this immaterial spirit, too, is not thought of as incorporeal but as invisible, gaseous. We thus come to the paradoxical view of God as an *ethereal vertebrate*.[4]

In fact, the real, sensory existence of a spiritual reality can be assumed only where an immediate sensory experience reveals the spirit, and spirit can be assumed only to the degree that it is perceived in this way. The great thinker Bartholomäus von Carneri (1821–1909) said:

> The words *no spirit without matter, but also no matter without spirit* would justify extending the problem to plants or even to the first rock we encounter, in which hardly anything could be said in favor of this correlation.[5]

Spiritual processes as facts are the results of various functions of an organism; the spirit of the world does not exist in the world in a material way but in a spiritual way only. The human soul is the sum of the processes in which spirit appears most directly *as a fact*. But it is *only* in the human being that spirit exists as such a soul. To look for spirit as a soul anywhere but in a human being—to view other beings as endowed with a soul like that of a human being— is to misunderstand spirit; it is to commit the most grievous sin

---

4. Ernst Haeckel, *The Riddle of the Universe* (Berlin, 1899), p. 333.
5. Bartholomäus von Carneri, *Empfindung und Bewusstsein* ("Sensation and consciousness," Bonn, 1893), p. 15.

against the spirit. Those who make this mistake reveal that they have not experienced spirit itself but only an external manifestation of spirit that rules in them—that is, the soul. It is as if somebody were to mistake a circle drawn in pencil for the true mathematical ideal circle. Those who experience within themselves only a soul form of spirit feel the need to assume such a soul form in nonhuman things so that they do not have to stop at gross sensory materiality. Instead of conceiving of the primordial foundation of the world as spirit, they think of it as a world soul and assume a general animation of nature.

Under the impact of the new Copernican view of nature, Giordano Bruno could grasp the spirit in the world (from which it had been driven in its old form) only as a *world soul*. Those who immerse themselves in Bruno's writings (especially in his profound book *Cause, Principle and Unity*), have the impression that he conceived of things as animated, though to various degrees. He had not really experienced spirit within himself and thus imagined it in terms of the human soul, the only form in which it confronted him. When he speaks of the spirit, he understands it in this way. "Universal reason is the most inward and real and characteristic faculty, and it is a potential part of the world soul; it is the same everywhere and fills the all-in-all; it illuminates the universe and instructs nature in producing its species as they should be." It is true that in these sentences the spirit is not described as an "ethereal vertebrate" but as a being like the human soul. "A thing, however minute, has within itself a portion of spiritual substance that, if it finds the substratum to be suitable, strives to become a plant or an animal and organizes itself into some kind of body, which is generally considered animated. Spirit may be found in all things, and there is not the most minute body that does not contain such a portion of it that it animates itself."

Because Giordano Bruno had not really experienced spirit as such within himself, he could confuse the life of spirit with those outer mechanical functions by means of which Ramon Llull (1235–1315), in his so-called "Great Art," had attempted to unveil the mysteries of the spirit.[6] The modern philosopher Franz Brentano described "Great Art": "Various concepts were inscribed on concentric, circular disks that can be turned individually, and in this way diverse combinations were produced."[7] A coincidence superimposed on a particular turn was formed into a judgment concerning the highest truths. In his extensive wanderings throughout Europe, Giordano Bruno appeared at various universities as a teacher of the "Great Art." He was bold enough to conceive of the stars as worlds completely analogous to our Earth. He enlarged the vision of scientific thinking beyond the Earth; he no longer thought of the *heavenly bodies* as *corporeal spirits* but thought of them as spirits of the *soul*. One must not do an injustice to this man whom the Catholic Church put to death for his advanced ideas. It was an enormous achievement to enfold the whole heavens within the same concept of the world that until then had been applied only to the earthly things (though Bruno still conceived of the sensory realm as belonging to the soul).

* * *

IN THE SEVENTEENTH CENTURY, the thinker Johannes Scheffler (called Angelus Silesius) made the visions of Tauler, Weigel, Jacob Boehme, and others shine once more in a great spiritual

---

6. Ramon Llull (or Ramond Lully, 1235–1316), Catalan mystic, philosopher, poet, and missionary. After an early life at the court of Majorca as a lyrical troubadour, he experienced mystical visions and left court to devote himself to philosophy and missionary work. He traveled in Asia Minor and North Africa in attempts to convert Muslims. According to legend, he was stoned to death. As a philosopher, he was primarily a neo-Platonic Aristotlian. His main work was *Ars magna*.

7. Franz Brentano, *Die vier Phasen der Philosophie und ihr augenblicklicher Stand* (Stuttgart, 1895), p. 20; Brentano (1838–1917) was a German philosopher and professor in Würzburg and Vienna; he presented his ideas on "act psychology," or intentionalism, Aristotle, logic, and ethics in books such as *Psychologie von empirischen Standpunkte* (1874) and *Von der Klassifikation der psychische Phänomene* (1911); see Steiner's *Riddles of the Soul*, chapter 3, "Franz Brentano, in Memoriam."

harmony.[8] The ideas of the older thinkers appear in his book *Cherubinic Wanderer* as though gathered in a spiritual focus and shining with a heightened luminosity. Everything Silesius said appears as a direct and spontaneous revelation of his personality, making it seem as though he was destined by providence to embody wisdom in a personal form. The spontaneous way his life expressed that wisdom is shown in his sayings, which may be admired as well for their artistic quality. He hovered above earthly existence like a spiritual being, and what he said is like a breath from another world, cleansed entirely of all those coarse and impure elements that human wisdom must struggle to leave behind.

In the philosophy of Angelus Silesius, only those who cause the eye of the all-in-all to see within them may partake of true cognition, and only those who feel that their acts are performed by the hand of the all-in-all may see them in their true light:

> God is the fire within me, and I am the light in him. Do we not belong to each other intimately?... I am as rich as God. There is no grain of dust that I do not have in common with him; dear people, believe me.... God loves me above himself. If I love him above myself, I give him as much as he gives me.... The bird is in the air, the stone lies on the land, the fish lives in the water, and my spirit is in God's hand.... If you are born of God, then God flowers in you, and his divinity is your sap and adornment.... Stop! What are you chasing after? Heaven is within you. If you are looking for God anywhere else, you will always miss him.[9]

For those who feel that they exist in the all-in-all in this way, all separation between themselves and other beings cease. Such people

---

8. Johannes Scheffler, or Angelus Silesius (1624–1677), Polish mystic, polemicist, and poet, was trained as a physician and ordained a Catholic priest. He spoke vigorously for the Counter-Reformation. The *Cherubinic Wanderer* (six vols.) is his important written work.
9. *Cherubinic Wanderer*, vol. 1: 11, 14, 18, 80, 81, 82.

no longer view themselves as separate individuals; on the contrary, they feel everything about themselves is a part of the world and that their true essence is identical with the universe itself:

> The world does not hold you. Rather, you are the world that, within you and with you, keeps you so powerfully imprisoned — You will not have perfect bliss until oneness has swallowed the otherness. — You are all things; if you lack one thing, you do not know your true wealth.[10]

As sensory beings, we are "things" among other things, and our sensory organs give us, as sensing individualities, information about the objects outside us in space and time. When spirit speaks in us, however, outside and inside cease to exist. Nothing spiritual is here or there, earlier or later. Space and time disappear in contemplating universal spirit. Only when we see as individuals are we "here" and the thing "there"; only when we see as individuals is one thing earlier and another later:

> Friends, when you let your spirit rise above place and time, you can be in eternity every moment. — I myself am eternity when I leave time and collect myself in God and God in myself. — The rose that your outer eye sees here has flowered like this in God through eternity. — Sit in the center, and you will see everything at once, what happens both now and then, both here and in Heaven. — My friend, as long as place and time is in your mind, you will never comprehend the nature of God and eternity. — When we withdraw from multiplicity and commune with God, we attain oneness.[11]

Here we climb to the heights that go beyond individual self and abolish every distinction between world and self. A higher life

---

10. Ibid., vol. 2:85; vol. 4:10; vol. 1:140.
11. Ibid., vol. 1:12, 13, 108; vol. 2:183; vol. 4:215, 224.

begins. The inner experience that arises appears as the death of our old life and a resurrection in the new:

> When you rise above yourself and let God act, then the Ascension will take place in your spirit —The body must elevate itself in the spirit, the spirit in God, if you, dear friend, wish to live in him forever in bliss. — To the degree that my I pines away and diminishes in me, the I of the Lord is strengthened.[12]

It is from this point of view that people can understand their significance and that of everything in the realm of eternal necessity. The natural universe appears to them directly as divine spirit. The thought of a divine, universal spirit that could have its being and continuity above and along side the things of the world disappears as a conquered concept.

This universal spirit seems to permeate things so completely and has become so entirely one with their nature that it is no longer possible to imagine even a single aspect of its being as absent. "There is nothing but I and you; if we two do not exist, then God is God no more, and the heavens shall fall." (*ibid.*, vol. 2:178) Human beings feel themselves to be a necessary link in the chain of the world. Their acts no longer have any element of arbitrariness or individuality. What they do is necessary to the whole, to the chain of the world, which would fall apart if what they do were taken out of it:

> Without me, God cannot make a single worm. If I do not preserve it with him, it must straightway fall to pieces. — I know that without me God cannot live for an instant. If I come to nothing, he must give up the ghost.[13]

---

12. Ibid., vol. 4:56; 5:88, 126.
13. Ibid., vol. 1:96, 8.

It is only on this height that people see things in their true nature. They no longer need to attribute a spiritual essence externally to the smallest, coarsest phenomena. In all its smallness and its gross, sensory nature, it is a part of the all-in-all.

> No dust mote is so poor, no dot is so small, but the wise person sees God in it in his glory. — In a mustard seed, if you can understand it, is the image of all higher and lower things.[14]

At this level of understanding, a person feels free, because coercion exists only where one can still be compelled externally. When everything outside has flowed into the interior, when the contrast between "I and world," "outside and inside," "nature and spirit" has disappeared; then, only their own impulses are experienced as compelling:

> Bind me as tight as you like, in a thousand irons; I will nevertheless be completely free and unfettered. — When my will is dead, then God must do my will. I myself prescribe for him the pattern and the goal.[15]

All externally imposed moral norms cease to exist. Human beings become their own measure and goal. They are not subject to any law, because the law, too, has become their own nature. "The law is for the wicked. If no commandment were written, the godly would nevertheless love God and their neighbors." (*ibid.*, vol. 5:277) On the higher level of cognition, the innocence of nature is returned to the human being. People accomplish the tasks assigned to them with the awareness of an eternal necessity. They say to themselves that, through this iron necessity, it is given into their hands to withdraw the part that is assigned to them from the same eternal necessity:

---

14. Ibid., vol. 4:160, 161.
15. Ibid., vol. 1:118, 98.

Dear people, let the flower in the meadow show you how to please God and be beautiful at the same time. — The rose does not ask why. It blooms because it blooms. It pays no attention to itself nor does it wonder if anyone sees it.[16]

When we rise to a higher level of understanding, we feel within ourselves the eternal and necessary impulse of the universe, just like the flower of the field; we act just as the flower does in blooming. In all our actions, the awareness of our moral responsibility grows into the infinite. What we fail to do is withdrawn from the all-in-all; it kills this all-in-all insofar as it is possible to kill the all-in-all:

What does it mean not to sin? Do not ask much. Go. The silent flowers will tell you. — Everything must be slain. If you do not slay yourself for God, eternal death will eventually slay you for the enemy.[17]

---

16. Ibid., vol. 1:288, 289.
17. Ibid., vol. 3:98; vol. 5:193.

Epilogue

ALMOST TWO AND A HALF CENTURIES have passed since Angelus Silesius gathered in *Cherubinic Wanderer* the profound wisdom of his precursors. Those centuries have brought rich insights into nature. Goethe opened a vast perspective into natural science. He pursued the eternally fixed laws of nature's work up to the peak where they produced humankind just as inevitability as, on a lower level, they produce stones.[1] Lamarck, Darwin, Haeckel, and others continued to work in the spirit of that thinking.

And the "question of questions" was answered in the nineteenth century—that is, What is the origin of humankind? Other questions in the realm of natural processes have also been solved. Today we know that it is unnecessary to go beyond the realm of facts and the senses to understand, in a purely natural way, the sequence of beings in human evolution. The nature of the human I, too, has been illuminated by the discernment of Johann Fichte, who showed the people where to look for the soul and described its nature.[2] Hegel extended the domain of thought to cover all fields of being and endeavored to comprehend in thought the outer, sensory existence of nature, as well as the highest creations of the human spirit and the laws that govern them.[3]

How do those men, whose thinking this work outlines, appear in light of a worldview that includes the scientific advancements of

---

1. See Rudolf Steiner, *Goethe's World View*.
2. See chapters 6 & 7 in *Riddles of Philosophy*.
3. See the presentation of Hegel in *Riddles of Philosophy*.

periods since theirs? They still believed in a "supernatural" history of creation. How do their thoughts appear in the face of "natural" views developed by nineteenth-century science? Science has not attributed anything to nature that does not belong there; it has removed from nature only what does not belong to it. Science ridded nature of everything that cannot be found there but only within the human being. Science no longer sees a force in nature that resembles the human soul and acts like a human being. It no longer proclaims an anthropomorphized God that *creates* organic forms, but describes their development in the sensory world strictly according to natural laws.

Meister Eckhart—as well as Johannes Tauler, Jacob Boehme, and Angelus Silesius—would feel profoundly at home contemplating natural science. When *understood properly*, one sees that the spirit of their worldview had developed fully into this view of nature. They could not illuminate the reality of nature through the light that arose within them, but this would have no doubt become their desire had natural science been available to them. They were unable to see nature in this light, because no geology and no "natural history of creation" informed them of those natural processes. Only the Bible spoke in its own way of such processes.

Thus, to the best of their ability, they looked for spirit in the only place it may be found—in the human being. Today they would use very different resources, by means accessible to the senses, to show that spirit may be found only in the human being. They would agree entirely with those who look for the reality of spirit not at the root of nature but in its fruit. They would admit that the spirit in the sensory body is the *result of development* and cannot be found at lower levels of development. They would understand that no "creative thought" is active in the forming spirit in an organism any more than creative thought caused apes to develop from marsupials.

In our own time, people cannot speak of natural facts as did Jacob Boehme. But today there is also a viewpoint that brings Boehme's thinking closer to a worldview that includes modern science. It is not necessary to lose the spirit when one finds only what is natural in nature. Of course, today there are many who think that one must slip into a shallow, dry materialism by accepting the discoveries of natural science at face value. I myself stand completely upon the ground of this natural science. I am convinced that a view of nature like that of Ernst Haeckel becomes shallow only when people approach it with a world of ideas that is already shallow. When I let the *revelations* of a "natural history of creation" affect me, I feel something higher and more glorious than when I confront the stories of supernatural miracles of the Creed. I know of nothing in "holy" books that reveals anything as sublime as the so-called dry fact that every human fetus rapidly progresses through a succession of all the forms through which its animal ancestors evolved.

Let us fill our minds with the magnificent facts that our senses perceive, and we will have little care for supernatural miracles. If we experience spirit within ourselves, we do not need spirit in external nature. In my *Intuitive Thinking as a Spiritual Path: A Philosophy of Freedom* I described my worldview, which does not eliminate spirit, because it views nature just as Darwin and Haeckel viewed it. A plant or an animal does not gain anything if I attribute to it a soul not perceived by my senses. I do not look for a deeper, spiritual nature of things in the external world; I do not even assume it, because I believe that the knowledge illuminating my inner self prevents me from doing so. I believe that things of the sensory world are as they appear to be, because I see that true self-knowledge leads us to look only for natural processes in nature. I do not look for divine spirit in nature, because I believe I perceive the essence of human spirit in myself. I calmly acknowledge my animal ancestors, because I realize that no soul-like spirit can be *active* in the origins of these animal ancestors. I agree with Ernst Haeckel only in his preference for the "eternal stillness of the grave" to the immortality of many religious doctrines.[4] I consider it to be a degradation and

---

4. See *Riddle of the Universe*.

an abhorrent sin *against spirit* to conceive of a soul that continues to exist like a sensory being.

I hear a shrill dissonance when the facts of natural science according to Haeckel encounter the pious creeds of many contemporaries. In creeds that harmonize poorly with natural facts I do not hear any of the spirit of the higher piety of Jacob Boehme and Angelus Silesius. That piety harmonizes fully with the activity of the natural world. There is no contradiction in being permeated with the insights of modern science and at the same time embarking upon the road that Boehme and Silesius pursued in their search for the spiritual. Those who take this road in the mode of those thinkers do not have to worry about slipping into shallow materialism as long as they allow the secrets of nature to be told by a natural history of creation. Those who interpret my ideas in this sense will understand as I do the last saying of the *Cherubinic Wanderer*, which will also sound the last note of this book.[5]

Dear friend, this is enough for now. If you wish to read more, go and become the writing and the essence yourself.[6]

---

5. This footnote was added to the 1923 edition: The final sentences should not be misinterpreted as expressing an *nonspiritual* view of nature. I wanted only to strongly emphasize that the spirit at the root of nature must be found *within* it and not to be brought to it externally. The rejection of "creative thoughts" refers to an activity like human activity, which acts according to ideas of utility. What is to be said about evolutionary history may be found in my preface to the new edition of *The Theory of Knowledge in Goethe's Conception of the World.*—RUDOLF STEINER, 1923.

6. *The Cherubinic* Wanderer, vol. 6:263.

About the Author, the People, and the Background of This Book

from the first edition

SHORTLY BEFORE the beginning of the twentieth century, Rudolf Steiner arrived in Berlin to assume the post of editor of the well-known *Magazin für Litteratur*, which had been established by Joseph Lehmann in 1832, the year of Goethe's death. Steiner was well-qualified for this position, having edited and written commentary on the natural scientific writings of Goethe for the Kurschner and the Weimar Editions of Goethe's works, a task for which he had been originally recommended by the celebrated Goethe scholar, Karl Julius Schröer, under whom Steiner had studied at the University of Vienna. Steiner also had edited the works of Schopenhauer and Jean Paul Richter for the well-known Cotta *Library of World Literature* series. Steiner's work as a writer for various periodicals in Vienna, Weimar, and Berlin included observations on current affairs, reviews of books and plays, and comment on scientific, social, and philosophical developments.

As an author in his own right, Steiner had already produced his *Theory of Knowledge Implicit in Goethe's World Conception* in 1886 at the age of twenty-five. In this book he revealed his comprehensive grasp of the deeper implications of Goethe's way of thinking. During his Weimar residence while working at the Goethe-Schiller Archives as a free collaborator on the Weimar edition of Goethe, Steiner developed lines of thought which he later expressed in *Goethe's Conception of the World*, published in 1897. These two works, together with his introductions and commentary on Goethe's scientific writings, established Steiner as one of the outstanding exponents of Goethe's methodology.

In 1891, Steiner received his Ph.D. at the University of Rostock. His thesis dealt with the scientific teaching of Fichte and is evidence of Steiner's ability to evaluate the work of men whose influence has gone far to shape the thinking of the modern world. In somewhat enlarged form, this thesis appeared under the title *Truth and Science* as the preface to Steiner's chief philosophical work, *Die Philosophie der Freiheit* (*Intuitive Thinking as a Spiritual Path: A Philosophy of Freedom*, 1894). Later he suggested *The Philosophy of Spiritual Activity* as the title of the English translation of this book.

Steiner's contact with the circle of Friedrich Nietzsche led to his work in the Nietzsche Archives and Library. Out of the profound impression the ideas of Nietzsche made upon him, he wrote his *Friedrich Nietzsche: Fighter for Freedom.*

With Steiner's arrival in Berlin, his lecturing activity, which had begun years before in Vienna, and had been continued in Weimar, was extended and increased. Eventually this work was to occupy the major portion of his time, and was to take him on repeated lecture tours throughout Western Europe. These journeys extended from Norway, Sweden, and Finland in the north to Italy and Sicily in the south, and included several visits to the British Isles. From about the turn of the century until his death in 1925, Steiner gave well over 6,000 lectures before audiences of the most diverse backgrounds and from every walk of life.

Steiner's written works, which eventually included over fifty titles, together with his extensive lecturing activity, brought him into contact with increasing numbers of people in many countries. The sheer physical and mental vigor required to carry on a life of such broad, constant activity is sufficient to mark him as one of the most creatively productive men of our time.

* * *

The present book, *Mystics after Modernism,* is a fruit of Steiner's lecturing activity. The substance of it was contained in a series of lectures he gave in Berlin beginning just after Michaelmas in 1900 when he was thirty-nine. Steiner wrote later, "By means of the ideas of the mystics from Meister Eckhart to Jacob Boehme, I found expression for the spiritual perceptions that, in reality, I decided to set forth. I then summarized the series of lectures in the book *Mystics after Modernism.*"

The term *mysticism,* as Steiner uses it in this book, is a development of what Goethe indicated in his aphoristic description of mysticism in relation to poetry and philosophy. "Poetry," said Goethe, "points to the riddles of nature and tries to solve them by means of the image. Philosophy directs itself to the riddles of reason and attempts to solve them by means of the word. Mysticism considers the riddles of both nature and reason and seeks to solve them through both word and image."

This book is significant in the life-work of Rudolf Steiner, because it is a first result of his decision to speak out in a direction not immediately apparent in his earlier, more philosophical writings, mentioned above. Here—particularly in Steiner's introduction—is a vitally fundamental exposition of the science of the spirit, embracing the path of spiritual knowledge suited to the needs and capacities of modern men and women. This subject occupied Steiner increasingly during the whole of the first quarter of this present century, and to it he devoted his entire talents as lecturer and writer.

* * *

Rudolf Steiner indicated that the present book is not intended to be a history of mysticism. It deals with a problem that had occupied him for decades, and which today has become a cardinal concern of all humankind: the impact of modern scientific thinking upon the experiences of our inner, spiritual life. In the conflict between reason and revelation which reached its climax in the nineteenth century, but that had its origins in much earlier times, Steiner saw the seed of a still greater conflict to come, a conflict that involves humanity's struggle against the sub-human in modern technical developments.

It is now generally realized that the impact of the atomic age challenges our inner convictions, our spiritual striving, and ultimately our ability to live a truly satisfying life.

In this book, Steiner tells how eleven men whose lives bridge the four centuries from the Gothic time to the mid-seventeenth century, solved the conflict between their inner spiritual perceptions and the world of individual freedom, invention, and discovery then coming to birth. He explains the positive contribution of their ideas to an understanding and preservation of the humanity of modern men and women in face of contemporary events.

In order that the reader may better appreciate Steiner's presentation of the leading thoughts of these men, a brief sketch of their times and their life stories is given in the following pages.

* * *

The period covered by the lives of the men whose ideas are discussed in this book links such diverse personalities as Dante Alighieri, who expressed the strivings of the Age of Faith in his *Divina Commedia*, and George Fox, whose experience of the inner light established the spiritual path of the Society of Friends in a century of skepticism and growing materialism. Great changes in human thinking took place in these four hundred years. The world of chivalry and knighthood, of pious hermit and wandering minstrel, of religious pilgrimage and miracle play, so characteristic of the medieval time, gave way to the new learning, the humanism, the centralized governments, the scientific investigation, the expanding horizons, both physical and mental, of the Renaissance. And no single part of human life was untouched by the change. In the political, religious, social, intellectual spheres the Renaissance worked its wonders, and the dream of the Middle Ages awakened to the glorious colors of the dawn of a new world.

The transformation in people's minds included a break with their former way of looking at the earth beneath their feet, at their fellow-men, and at the blue vault arching over their heads. From a conception of nature that saw the animate in everything even in stones—new systems of classification, ways of analysis, of explanation, based more and more upon the evidence of the physical senses, and less and less upon folk-lore and tradition, came into being. The new cosmopolitanism, the recovery of the art and philosophy of ancient Greece, and the breaking up of old parties and practices in the social and political life led ultimately to humanity's growing consciousness of *itself,* and of its intrinsic worth among other beings. The discovery of the shape of the earth, the rebirth of geographic learning lost in the dimness of forgotten ages, finally brought people to think of the possibility of worlds beyond this world, of whole solar systems beyond ours, and the word *infinite* began to assume a new importance. In the genius of language is revealed the momentous change that took place in these centuries. One need only recall that to the medieval mind the word *reality* referred exclusively to spiritual, heavenly things, to see how far reaching was the change that occurred at the dawn of the modern world.

Today, when modern technical developments have extended their sphere of activity to include interstellar space, and space travel is regarded as a rapidly approaching accomplishment, one can recall that to people of the Middle Ages even the high places of the earth itself were regarded with reverence as dwelling-places of Divinity. A Medieval man would have disliked even to approach high mountains, and to climb them would have required inconceivable daring. As Ruskin said, "Men of the Middle Ages believed that mountains were agreeable things enough, so long as they were far away."

With the rise of the new thinking of the Renaissance, however, people began to lose their awe of high mountains, and one of the pioneer mountain climbers was Petrarch, the Italian poet. With his brother Gherado, Petrarch climbed Mount Ventroux, a six thousand foot peak near Avignon, on April 26, 1336. All seems to have gone well until at the summit Petrarch discovered that the very clouds of heaven were beneath his feet. Overcome with excitement not unmixed with concern, he took out of his pocket the copy of Augustine's writings he always carried with him. Opening the book at random his eye fell upon a sentence which struck through him like lightning, for it sternly warned man never to lift his head out of the dust of earth, but always to remember his entire subservience to his Maker. Deeply moved, Petrarch descended the mountain filled with secret shame that he had had the temerity to trespass upon a place denied man by the teaching of the Church Fathers.

As people of the Middle Ages believed the mountains to be sacred, so they also regarded the human body as something set apart as the dwelling-place of our immortal soul. Therefore to them the anatomical studies practiced by Renaissance investigators like Leonardo da Vinci would have seemed blasphemous in the highest degree.

As people of the Renaissance learned to take possession of the earth with their thinking, they reached out to embrace its far places physically as well. The age of discovery and exploration was followed by a period of conquest and colonization.

Parallel with the humanistic impulses of the Renaissance ran the current of the Reformation, with the accompanying strife and violence of the Counter-Reformation. Finally, as the four centuries covered by the lives of the men considered in this book drew to a close, strong national states emerged, with cultural, political, and social activities closely interrelated.

The year Meister Eckhart was born, Louis IX, known to posterity as Saint Louis of France, leader of the last Crusade, died. When Angelus Silesius died, the *Grand Monarque*, Louis XIV, destined to rule France for seventy-two years, was thirty-nine years of age, in the full strength of his manhood.

From the foregoing can be seen that the period covered by the lives of these men is the time when humanity, particularly in the Western world, evolved into a condition of consciousness in which the things of the sense world dominated all other considerations, in contrast to the preceding age, when the things of the spirit prevailed to such an extent that no sacrifice of earthly things was considered too great if, for example, it would enhance the miraculous, heaven-aspiring glory of a rising Gothic cathedral.

1

In the year 1260 while Marco Polo was on his way to China, thus giving birth to new East–West relationships, and Niccolo Pisano was calling deathless beauty to life in his sculpture in Pisa, Johannes Eckhart was born in the little Thuringian village of Hochheim near Gotha in Germany. His father was a steward in a knight's castle, hence Johannes' boyhood was passed in the midst of the then fading pageantry of medieval life.

Eckhart was born in the time of transition between the end of the Hohenstaufen rule and the beginning of the reign of the Austrian Hapsburgs in Germany. The period of one hundred and sixteen years of Hohenstaufen rule (1138–1254) was probably the most interesting period in medieval Germany, and its influence was still active during Eckhart's boyhood, though the last Hohenstaufen had died six years before Eckhart's birth.

This was an age of great contrasts. On the one hand were men of strong, vigorous mind, filled with love for all that the world contained of beauty and adventure. On the other were men whose character was equally strong, but whose lives were spent in a continual struggle of rejection of the world and all its gifts. These were the years when these two opposed attitudes toward the world began a conflict which was to lead to the Renaissance in Germany and, at last, to the Reformation. Typical of the Hohenstaufen rulers was Frederick II, considered the most brilliant of all German kings. He was a lover of poetry, art, literature, and was a most capable ruler as well. Crowned at Aix-la-Chapelle in July, 1215, Frederick combined the traditional knightly ideals with worldly activity. The rule of the Hohenstaufens corresponded with the golden age of the German *Minnesinger* and was a time of architectural development, which included many beautiful churches as well as the famous castle of the Wartburg.

At about the age of fifteen, around the year 1275, Eckhart entered the Dominican monastery at Erfurt, where he remained for nine years in preparation for the priesthood. He completed his studies in the year that Philip IV, known as "the Fair," began his fateful reign in France.

From Erfurt, Eckhart went to Cologne to take the *studium generate* at the Dominican institution where the eminent scholastic, Albertus Magnus was a leading teacher until his death in 1280. Through his instructors at Cologne, Eckhart came under the influence of Albertus Magnus' ideas, as well as those of Thomas Aquinas, whose work had advanced Scholasticism to a place of first importance within the Dominican Order.

The year 1300 was famous as the Year of Jubilee proclaimed by Boniface VIII, whom Dante criticized by placing him in the *Inferno* during the Pope's lifetime. In this same year Eckhart is mentioned as "Brother Eckhart, Prior of Erfurt, Vicar of Thuringia" in Dominican records. He was now in his fortieth year, and about this time he produced a little book which bears the charming title, *Daz sint die rede der unterscheidunge, die der Vicarius von Düringen, der prior non Erfort, breeder Eckehart predier ordens mit solichen kinden hete, din in dirre rede frâgten vil dirges, do sie sâzen in collationibus mit einander* ("These are the instructions that the Vicar of Thuringia, Prior of Erfurt, Brother Eckhart of the Preaching Order, gave for those of his flock who asked him about many things as they sat together at the evening meal").

At this time Eckhart was sent to one of the colleges in Paris, where he frequently entered into disputation with Franciscans in defense of Dominican points of view in theology. In his disputations he had to defend the writings of Thomas Aquinas and Albertus Magnus against any charges of heresy which the Franciscans chose to bring forward against them.

Thirteenth-century Paris was a place of great attraction for scholars and the center of European cultural life. Over one hundred fifty years before, Pierre Abelard had written of his intense desire to visit Paris, the city where logical argumentation, beloved by the medieval scholarly mind, had been raised to the level of a fine art. John of Salisbury, Bishop of Chartres, eminent as a humanist long before the Renaissance, the secretary and counsellor of Thomas Becket of Canterbury, whose assassination he witnessed and whose life he recorded, loved Paris for its generous supply of food, the gaiety of its inhabitants, their appreciation of culture and religion, and the atmosphere of scholarship he found there. He summed up his feelings about Paris in the exclamation, "Indeed the Lord is in this place, and I did not know it!"

Years later Eckhart described his Paris activities in terms that perhaps explain why the Franciscans cherished no particular liking for him. With regard to his disputations with the Franciscans, Eckhart said, "When I preached at Paris, I said—and I dare repeat it now—that, with all their learning, the men of Paris are not able to conceive that God is in the very least of creatures—even in a fly!"

Words like these help one to understand Eckhart's popularity with the public of his time. For above all, Eckhart wished to reach the man in the street, the humble peasant, the shepherd from the mountains, the charcoal burner from the forest, the simplest of the simple, rather than the scholar in the cloister. Therefore he used colloquial German in all his writings and discourses rather than the usual theological Latin. Thus the German language was enhanced by the writings of this Dominican, just as the Italian language was enriched by his contemporary, Dante Alighieri.

Eckhart was always conscious of his indebtedness to the other great Dominicans who had preceded him, and although he did not follow their learned forms in his sermons and books, he never failed to recognize their superiority in learning. For example, his frequent quotations in his oral and written discourse were invariably introduced by the words, "A Master says," and the "Master" almost always meant Thomas Aquinas, whom he looked upon as a spiritual father. Though his genius for adapting learned, subtle arguments to simple, aphoristic form resulted in his being understood by the everyday mind, nevertheless this ultimately led to the condemnation of his teaching as heretical.

In 1302, the year after the famous Duns Scotus became professor of theology at Oxford, Eckhart received the Licentiate and Master's degree from the University of Paris. Ever since then he has been known as Meister Eckhart.

At this time Boniface VIII, who had been informed of the brilliant preaching of this Thuringian Dominican, invited Eckhart to Rome to defend the cause of the papacy against the attacks of the French king, Philip the Fair, which were soon to result in the "Babylonian Captivity" of the Popes at Avignon.

In 1304, the year of the birth of Petrarch, Eckhart was appointed provincial of the Dominicans for Saxony. Three years later he was appointed vicar-general for Bohemia, at the moment the arrest and terrible persecution of the Order of the Knights Templar began in France under the direction of Philip the Fair, and with the passive agreement of the French-born Pope, Clement V, who in the meanwhile had succeeded Boniface VIII in the papacy.

This was a busy period in the life of Meister Eckhart. His burden of administrative work in the service of the Church and of his Order was increased by his activity as a writer. At this time he composed one of his best-known works, *The Book of Divine Comfort*, supposedly written to bring consolation to Agnes, daughter of the King of Hungary, whose mother and sister-in-law died and whose father was murdered—all within the space of a few years.

The Book of Divine Comfort opens with an enumeration of the three kinds of tribulation Eckhart conceives may happen to one: damage to external goods, to friends near one, to oneself, bringing "disgrace, privation, physical suffering, and mental anguish" in their train. As "comfort" in the midst of such tribulation, Eckhart sets forth "certain doctrines" from which he derives "thirty teachings, any one of which should be enough to comfort." Whether the suffering of the Queen of Hungary was assuaged by Eckhart's effort on her behalf is not known, but the book brought Eckhart himself considerable tribulation, for it is his one work most strenuously attacked by the Inquisition. This book is evidence of Eckhart's careful study of the famous classic born in the twilight of the ancient Roman world, *The Consolations of Philosophy*, by Boethius, loved by Alfred the Great, who translated it into Anglo-Saxon; by Chaucer, who was to translate it into English before 1382; by Queen Elizabeth, who rendered it in the English of her time; and by many others. Aside from its theological teachings, his *Book of Divine Comfort* shows Eckhart's appreciation of Boethius and other classical writers.

The constant travel necessitated by his administrative work brought Eckhart into contact with people and events in central, southern and western Germany, in France, and in Italy. As a result, it is natural that the heads of the Order felt that Meister Eckhart was the ideal man to assume the post of Superior of the entire Dominican Province in Germany. However, a certain conservatism within the Order itself, apparently based on fear of Eckhart's skill as an orator and disputant, his broad knowledge of places, and familiarity with the ways of people in all walks of life prevailed, and his nomination was never finalized.

In 1318, the year that Dante completed his *Divina Commedia*, Eckhart seems to have reached the summit of his development as a preacher. He was in Strassburg at this time, where he served as a preacher and prior. Two years later, in 1320, at the age of sixty, Eckhart received a most important honor: he was called by the Franciscan, Heinrich van Virneberg, Archbishop of Cologne, to assume a professorship in the college there. However, the brightness of this distinction was not long to remain undimmed. Already in the shadows the agents of the Inquisition waited, listening, watching, preparing for the day when this eloquent preacher of the Gospel, this scholar and author, so beloved by the common people who flocked to his sermons, would overstep the limits of prescribed dogma. And it was not long before they believed that they had evidence sufficient to convict him of heresy.

By 1325 several charges had been brought against Meister Eckhart in letters addressed to the Superiors of the Dominican Order at its headquarters in Venice. A few months later, the Archbishop of Cologne who already had had sufficient trouble with so-called "mystical societies" that had sprung up along the Rhine in areas under his jurisdiction, decided that heresy certainly could not be allowed to set foot within the precincts of the college itself. Therefore he agreed that the moment had arrived when charges against this too-popular preacher should be laid before the Inquisition. However, a fellow-Dominican managed to obtain the task of investigating Meister Eckhart, and naturally it did not take long for the former to report that he found Eckhart entirely without guilt or taint of heresy.

But the matter did not stop there. Perhaps sensing that if Franciscans had undertaken the examination things might have turned out differently, the Archbishop called in two experts in heresy, the Franciscans Benherus Friso and Peter de Estate. They were given the task to thoroughly examine Eckhart's writings and the reports of his sermons. It was not long before an extensive list of "errors" in doctrine had been assembled, and Eckhart in turn replied by means of his famous "defense" (*Rechtfertigungsschrift*).

On January 24, 1327, Eckhart was required to answer the charges brought against him before the court of the Archbishop of Cologne. About three weeks later he preached in a Cologne church in defense of his ideas, and said that if there were any errors of faith in his writings or sermons, he would retract them gladly, for he certainly considered himself no heretic, and he appealed to Rome, as he was entitled to do under the rights of his order. However, on February 22, Eckhart was informed that his application to Rome had been refused.

On March 27, 1329, Pope John XXII issued a bull describing certain of Meister Eckhart's teachings as contrary to church dogma. But Eckhart was no longer alive to know of his condemnation as one who had been led astray "by the father of lies, who often appears as an angel of light." This official fiat would doubtless have seriously shaken the soul of one whose life had been devoted to a defense and practice of the tenets from which that organized power had drawn its life-breath.

2

When Meister Eckhart was forty years of age, Johannes Tauler was born in the city of Strassburg in the Papal Jubilee year of 1300, two years before the death of the painter, Cimabue. At the age of fifteen he entered the Dominican monastery where Eckhart was professor of theology. One can imagine the effect of the older Dominican teacher upon the impressionable mind of the young student, who well may have listened to those evening mealtime conversations Eckhart brought together in the little book mentioned above. Eventually Tauler entered the Dominican college in Cologne not long before Eckhart was named professor in that institution.

The year 1324 saw the climax of a struggle between Louis IV, king of Germany, and Pope John XXII, which had been increasing steadily for nearly a decade. Fearing that the German king's policy of personal ambition would lead to a weakening of the papal position in France as well as Germany, the Pope called upon the German ruler to abdicate, saying that no one could rightfully wear the German crown who did not have the Pope's express approval to do so. Louis angrily refused, with the result that the Pope declared him deposed and excommunicate. Therefore, in this year 1324, Strassburg, along with other cities and towns of Germany, was placed under a papal interdict.

But the times were against the Pope and his French ally, Charles IV, whom he hoped to see on the German throne. The German princes condemned in no uncertain terms the papal interference in German affairs, and the electors sided with the princes. This attitude was also shared by many of the clergy in Germany, for despite the papal ban, church services continued in some places, and the sacraments were administered to the people.

Johannes Tauler was among those in Strassburg who refused to discontinue their priestly functions of celebrating the Mass and preaching to their congregations. With great courage, in defiance of both papal ban and agents of the Inquisition, he said, "While the

Church can refuse us the sacrament externally, nobody can take away the spiritual joy of our oneness with God, and nobody can rob us of the privilege of taking the sacrament spiritually."

In 1339, the year before the birth of Geoffrey Chaucer in London, Tauler left Strassburg for a journey which was to have important results for his life work. On his travels he came into contact—particularly in Basel—with Swiss and German members of the famous group of mystics called the *Gottesfreunde* (the Friends of God).

The struggle for power between rival rulers in Germany, together with the interdict of the Pope, brought great hardship to the people. Some areas of the country were not freed from the papal ban for as much as twenty-six years, and the people were in great distress for lack of spiritual help and consolation.

Abnormal phenomena also began to appear, as though the forces of nature had joined with spiritual and temporal rulers to make the lot of humankind as hard as possible. Torrential rains repeatedly destroyed the crops just before harvest time. Rivers rose in devastating floods several years in succession, making spring planting difficult, if not impossible. Winters were severely cold, so that both humans and animals suffered exceedingly. As a consequence, a series of famines swept the countryside, taking a dreadful toll of human life.

Convinced that they were living in the "last days" of the earth, many people saw in all the events around them the fulfillment of prophecies of the Apocalypse of John. During these years southern Germany and Switzerland were visited by repeated earthquakes, one of which shook Basel with such force that the city was reduced to a heap of ruins. In the heavens appeared "signs and wonders" prophesied by the Scriptures: mysterious lights flashed upon the skies, there were strange conditions of cloud and mist, and the stars seemed about to cast themselves upon the earth.

Visited by these dire external events, harassed by doubt and insecurity on every side, many withdrew more and more into themselves, seeking the sources of piety and devotion in their hearts. Lacking spiritual consolation from the church, suffering the desolation wrought by flood and famine, sword and fire, the people sought the essential truths of life in their personal experience. And in their search for the verities of existence, they reached out to one another in fraternal love and a spirit of true humanity.

Thus the Friends of God came into being. It was a free association of human beings in the sense that it was not a sect, had no dogma, no common form of religious devotion or practice, no common political outlook. The only desire the Friends of God shared in common was to strengthen one another in their living relationship with God and the spiritual world. They established "brotherhood houses" as retreat centers in certain areas where a number of the Friends of God were living.

One of the outstanding figures among the Friends of God was the wealthy banker of Strassburg, Rulman Merswin. His story is somewhat typical of that of many another layman who found himself drawn to the Friends of God. Born of a good family of Strassburg in 1307, Rulman Merswin was a man of business and high moral and ethical principles. By the time he was forty, due to his business acumen he had amassed a considerable fortune, and had married the daughter of one of the leading families of Strassburg. But although he had everything to give him pleasure, he was far from happy, and just after his fortieth birthday he decided that the time had come for him to take leave of the world, to devote himself and his wealth to the service of God, and to live as a celebate. His wife joined him on his mystical path. A few months later, on the day of Saint Martin, November 11, 1347, Merswin was walking in his garden in the evening, meditating on the way he and his wife had chosen, when suddenly he experienced a tremendous feeling of exaltation so that, as he later described it, it was as though he was whirled round and round his garden for sheer joy. But as quickly as the mood of exaltation came upon him, it left, and he slipped into a condition of despondency bordering upon despair. He began severe ascetic disciplines with the thought that these might relieve his inner struggle, but no light came.

At this time Johannes Tauler became his confessor, and Merswin told him of his suffering and his ascetic practices. Tauler at once forbade him to continue his self-imposed tortures, saying, "We are told to kill our passions, not our flesh and blood." Merswin obeyed, and only a short while later a Friend of God came to him and led him forward on the road to the spirit. He learned to depend quietly upon the guidance of the spirit alone, to subject himself to no code or rule of conduct, but to cultivate true humility, to seek anonymity, to cease self-assertion, to regard himself as a "captive of the Lord," to preserve the calmness of his soul like a stainless mirror, to attach less and less importance to himself in a worldly sense, and to think of himself only as "a hidden child of God."

On October 9, 1364, Rulman Merswin had a dream in which he was told that a most important man would shortly visit him, and that in three years he would purchase land which would make a home of peace and rest for the Friends of God in Strassburg. Not long after this, Merswin was visited by a mysterious man whose name is most intimately connected with the whole story of the Friends of God. Called simply the "Friend of God from the Oberland," he was long identified with the famous Nicholas of Basel, a noted Friend of God, who suffered martyrdom at the stake in Vienna for his convictions. Others have identified him with Rulman Merswin himself, as a sort of "double," while others believe that he never lived at all, but was a kind of ideal portrait of what the true Friend of God should be.

In any case, the Friend of God from the Oberland visited Merswin and told him that he had had a dream that Merswin would establish a retreat for the Friends of God at Strassburg. Merswin told him that he himself had had the same dream, and the Friend of God from the Oberland told him to wait quietly, to listen for the guidance of the Holy Spirit, and that at the end of three years he would know what was to be done.

In the Ill River near Strassburg was a little island called the Green Island (*daz Grüne Woerth*). In the twelfth century a convent had been established there, but had long since been deserted and had fallen into ruins. Early in October, 1367—just three years after his dream and his talk with the Friend of God from the Oberland—

Merswin was walking by the river and saw the little island. Suddenly the realization flashed through him that this was the place he was to buy, that here he was to establish a house for the Friends of God. He promptly sought out the owner, paid him five hundred and ten silver marks as the purchase price, and soon the convent building was repaired and a little chapel was constructed. Finally, on November 25, 1367 Merswin opened the house of the Friends of God on the Green Island, which became the center of a group of laymen who wished to live a purely mystical, religious life but without subjecting themselves to any external rule or official religious Order. Five years later Merswin completed arrangements whereby the group was acknowledged as a branch of the Knights of Saint John of Jerusalem, and the place became known as "The House of Saint John of the Green Island." Not long after this Merswin's wife died, and he spent his remaining years on the Green Island, devoting himself to the Friends of God who came there from far and near. Rulman Merswin died in the House of St. John of the Green Island on July 18, 1382. Four days after his death a sealed chest was opened which had been discovered in his room. Inside was a collection of manuscripts and letters, many of them in an unknown handwriting, giving details of instructions and advice by the Friend of God from the Oberland.

One of these manuscripts contained "The Story of the Master of Holy Scripture," later included in a collection titled, *The Great Memorial.* According to the "Story of the Master of Holy Scripture," the Friend of God from the Oberland one day arrived at a great city where a famous preacher was expounding the Bible to crowded and enthusiastic congregations. The Friend of God attended the sermons each day for five days. At the conclusion of the fifth day, he sought out the preacher and asked, "Reverend Sir, will you preach tomorrow on a theme I would suggest to you?" The clergyman agreed, and asked what the subject should be. The Friend of God from the Oberland replied, "How to attain the highest degree of spiritual life." The preacher delivered a brilliant exposition the next morning. Starting from the Gospels, he branched out into the Church Fathers, dipped deep into Dionysius, and concluded with a tremendous display of erudition. The congregation was enthralled by his words, but at the end of the service the theologian saw the Friend of God walk away silently and alone, with head bowed as though in deep thought.

The next day the Friend of God went to the clergyman and gave him a scathing criticism of the sermon, even saying that if that was the best he could do, then he was not capable of teaching about the spiritual life at all. The preacher's anger knew no bounds, but suddenly an inner voice told him to calm himself and to listen to the stranger's words. Having regained possession of himself once more, he quietly asked the Friend of God what help he could give him. Then the layman gave the Master of the Holy Scriptures twenty-three sentences, saying, "These are the ABC of religion; master these, and events will show their worth." The theologian withdrew from active service and spent a long time in meditation and prayer. His power of preaching left him, so that he could hardly speak an intelligible sentence, let alone deliver a whole sermon. His congregations deserted him; everywhere he was scorned and ridiculed.

After two years he was led by an inner voice that told him to enter the pulpit to preach during the service. Quietly he did so, noting the scorn and derision on the faces of the people as he faced them. For a long moment there was silence, then suddenly without any premeditation at all he gave out as his text, "Behold the Bridegroom cometh; go ye out to meet him!" And the spiritual power that flowed with his words was so great that it is said that forty persons fainted from sheer excitement and joy.

Tradition has long connected the "Master of Holy Scripture" with Johannes Tauler, and indicates that this is the account of his meeting with the Friend of God from the Oberland. Tauler became intimately acquainted with leading Friends of God in many places on his travels, and was deeply impressed with their way of life. As he said in a sermon at about this time, "The theologians of Paris study great tomes and turn over many pages, but the Friends of God read the living Book where everything is life."

Among the Friends of God whom Tauler met were Henry of Nördlingen, one of the outstanding representatives of the mysticism of the time, Hermann of Fritzlar, and two pious nuns, Christina Ebner, prioress of the Engelthal Convent near Nuremberg, and Margaretha Ebner, of the Convent of Maria Medingen in Swabia. One of the letters from the famous correspondence between Henry of Nördlingen and Margaretha Ebner is dated 1348, and asks that she "pray for Tauler, who lives as a matter of course in the midst of great trial and testing because he teaches the truth and lives in conformity with it as perfectly as a preacher can."

Having visited Friends of God in many places during his seven years' absence from Strassburg, Tauler was convinced that a layman has tasks to perform which basically are as spiritually important as those of the clergy. In one of his sermons Tauler reflects the religious-social spirit he had found in the way of life of the Friends of God: "One can spin, another can make shoes, and all these are gifts of the Holy Ghost. I tell you, if I were not a priest, I would esteem it a great gift that I was able to make shoes, and I would try to make them so well that they would be a model to all."

One of the documents which has come down to us from the Friends of God is a public announcement which probably originated in Strassburg, and may have been written by Rulman Merswin himself. It was copied and recopied, and was circulated very widely in southern and western Germany during Tauler's lifetime. It is of interest because it gives a picture of the kind of appeal which was made to the public by the Friends of God in their search for others who might be minded to join them:

"All those in whom the love of God or the terror brought about by the dreadful calamities of the present wakens a wish to begin a new and spiritual life, will discover great advantage in withdrawing into themselves every morning when they waken, in order to consider what they will do during the day. Should they find any evil thought in themselves, any purpose which is contrary to the divine will, let them give it up and cast it aside, to the glory of God. In the evening, upon going to bed, let them consider how they have spent the day. Let them recall what deeds they have done, and in what spirit they have performed them. If they discover that they have done any good, let them thank God, and give Him the glory. If they discover they have done evil, let them take the blame for it themselves, and lay the fault on nobody else, and let them deeply repent before God, saying to Him, 'O Lord, be merciful to me, and forgive all my sins of this day, for I sincerely repent, and I firmly intend from now on with Thy help, to avoid sinning.'"

In 1348 Strassburg was visited by the Black Death. All who could, fled the city, and soon few except the sick were left behind. Even relatives, nurses and physicians left for fear of the pestilence. But among those who stayed in the city to care for the sick, to comfort the dying, and to bury the dead, was Johannes Tauler.

Week after week, month after month, this fearless Dominican stood in his pulpit in defiance of papal ban and the Black Death and bore witness to the truth that was in him. In one of his sermons He pointed out that "In all the world God desires and requires but one thing: that He find the noble ground he has laid in our noble souls bare and ready, so that He may do His noble divine work therein." Hence it is necessary that we "let God prepare our ground, and give ourselves wholly to God and put away the self in all things."

But Tauler had no illusions about the trials that await us on our path of purification, on our way to the spirit: "When our heavenly Father determines to grace a particular soul with spiritual gifts, and to transform it in a special way, He does not purge it gently. Instead, He plunges it into a sea of bitterness, and deals with it as He did with the prophet Jonah."

He knew that "no teacher can teach what he has not lived through himself," and he continued his work at Strassburg against all odds, encouraging others by his Christianity in action. He had said, "Never trust a virtue which has not been put into practice." Now he was practicing the virtue of a Friend of God, the virtue of devotion to his fellow-men. It is no wonder that Luther was to write of him, "Never in either the Latin or German language have I found more wholesome, purer teaching, nor any that more fully agrees with the Gospel." Tauler's words were tried and purified in the fire of personal experience.

It is related that the Friend of God from the Oberland gave Tauler two prayers which he was to use every morning and evening. They are significant examples of the spirit which animated the mystical striving of the Friends of God. "In the morning you are to say, 'O Lord, I wish to keep from all sin today. Help me to do everything I do today according to Thy divine will and to Thy glory, whether my *nature* likes it or not.' In similar fashion every evening you are to say, 'O Lord, I am a poor, unworthy creature. Be merciful to me, forgive my sins, for I repent of them and sincerely desire Thy help that I may commit no more.'"

Tauler's writings have great appeal even today because of their freshness, their closeness to everyday life, their common sense. They are not primarily Scholastic speculations like much of Eckhart's writing, but are nearer to the vigorous directness of the Reformers. Although Tauler loved, as he described it, "to put out into the deep and let down the nets" into the world of study and meditation, at the same time he cautioned that such "spiritual enjoyments are food of the soul, and are only to be taken for nourishment and support to help us in our active work." This thought was echoed in the spirit of the Reformation.

In the years following the Black Death and the papal ban, Tauler continued to make Strassburg the center of his work. He kept up his correspondence with many of the Friends of God, especially with Margaretha Ebner. His services were crowded, and his sermons were held in the highest regard by his congregations.

On the fifteenth of June, 1361, in the Convent of Saint Nikolaus in Strassburg, Johannes Tauler died at the age of sixty-one. Tradition relates that for him the moment of death was an experience of pure joy, for as he said in one of his last sermons, "Eternity is the everlasting Now."

3

Linked with the name of Johannes Tauler as a Friend of God and a continuer of the work of Meister Eckhart is that of yet another Dominican, Heinrich Suso. Suso was born in 1295, five years before the birth of Tauler, in the town of Überlingen on the Lake of Constance (Bodensee). When he was still a small boy his parents decided he should study for the Church, and his preparatory education began at Constance, and was continued at Cologne, where he came under the influence of the teaching of Meister Eckhart.

Suso has revealed himself in his autobiography as a deeply emotional man, with a very unusual gift of expression. In his "glowing, vivid language," as it has been described, Suso pictured his mystical experiences in great detail, in contrast to the silence in which many other mystics have shrouded their strivings.

At about the age of eighteen, in 1313, the year Boccaccio was born in Florence, Suso entered a monastery in Constance. There he voluntarily subjected himself to the most severe ascetic ordeals. He centered his affection in an ideal which he personified under the name of the Eternal Wisdom. He relates how this figure appeared before him and said, "My son, give me your heart." He took a knife and cut deep into his chest the letters of the name Jesus, so that the scar-traces of each of the letters remained all his life, "about the length of a fingerjoint," as he says.

Suso once saw a vision of angels, and asked them in what manner God dwelt in his soul. The angel told him to look within. He did so, and as he gazed he saw that "his body over his heart was as clear as crystal, and in the center sat tranquilly, the lovely form of the Eternal Wisdom. Beside her sat, filled with heavenly longing, the servitor's own soul, which, leaning lovingly toward God's side, and encircled by His arms, lay pressed close to His heart." Suso wrote his autobiography in the third person, and referred to himself as the "servitor of the Divine Wisdom," much as Swedenborg in a later century was to refer to himself in his writings as "the servant of the Lord Jesus Christ."

Heinrich Suso took the expression, "No cross, no crown," with terrible literalness. He imposed fearful penances upon himself, and consumed sixteen long years in cruel austerity. For example, he relates how he donned a hair shirt, and bound himself with a heavy iron chain, but at length he had to give these up, since the loss of blood they occasioned was too much for his strength to bear. Instead he fashioned a crude night-shirt which he wore next to his skin. In this garment he sewed a series of leather straps in which sharp tacks were fitted so that they pierced his skin with his slightest movement. Later he made a cross of wood as tall as himself, and the cross-beam the length of his outstretched arms. Into this he drove thirty nails, and wore the cross fastened to his bare back, the nails pointing into his flesh. He bore this instrument of torture for some eight years, day and night. Finally, after sixteen years of agony, Suso had a vision at Whitsuntide in which he was assured that God no longer wished him to continue his austerities. Only then did he abate the severity of his asceticism, and threw his instruments of self-torture into a running stream near the monastery.

In his autobiography Suso relates that one time he prayed that God would instruct him how to suffer. In response, he had a vision of Christ on the cross in the likeness of a seraphic being with six wings. On each pair of wings the legend was inscribed, "Receive suffering willingly; Bear suffering patiently; Learn suffering in the way of Christ."

The result of this almost unbelievable "receiving, bearing, learning" of suffering was a man whose gentleness and calm, lyric beauty of speech won hearts to his teaching. The fires of affliction had nearly consumed him to ashes, yet, phoenix-like, his spirit rose anew in a sweetness of expression and a grandeur of soul which one could scarcely resist. In 1335, the year Giotto began his work on the Cathedral at Florence, Suso set out on his wanderings through Swabia as a traveling preacher. He advanced the spiritual teachings of Eckhart, but through his mystical fervor they were permeated by a newness, a spontaneous grace, and a transcendent beauty. And something of this spirit which was reborn in Suso comes down to us today in his autobiography, issued in 1365, which has established itself as a unique work of its kind, and as "one of the most interesting and charming of all autobiographies." Suso's preaching was especially popular among the nuns of the convents he visited. Their hearts were deeply impressed by the obvious, overwhelming sincerity and fervor of his manner and words.

Heinrich Suso's writings are among the classics of mysticism. His first work, *The Little Book of Truth*, was written in Cologne in 1329, and springs directly from the mystical teachings of Meister Eckhart. Somewhat later, in Constance he wrote of the more practical aspects of mysticism in his *Little Book of Eternal Wisdom*. This book has been called the "finest fruit of German mysticism.'

Something of the romanticism of the troubadour of the Ages of Faith, the charm of days gone by, the sad evanescence of the dream of chivalry, and the heroic ideals of knighthood lives in the mystical expressions of Suso. He developed a mood of gentleness, of tender, delicate imagery which set him apart from all the other men whose lives we are considering here.

Concerning his books, Suso wrote, "Whoever will read these writings of mine in a right spirit can hardly fail to be stirred in his heart's depths, either to fervent love, or to new light, or to longing and thirsting for God, or to detestation and loathing of his sins, or to that spiritual aspiration by which the soul is renewed in grace." These words gain "fearful symmetry," to use Blake's phrase, when we recall that they were written by one who, for example, had practiced such abstinence in eating and drinking, that often as he stood with his brother monks in choir at Compline, when the holy water was sprinkled over the group during the service, he opened his parched mouth toward the aspergillum in the hope that even a single drop of water might cool his burning thirst. Such a man can write about "longing and thirsting" as very few who have walked this earth have been able to do.

About 1348, his wandering in central and southern Germany having come to an end, this love-inspired Swabian poet-knight of the spirit, singer of the glories of Eternal Wisdom, settled at last in

Ulm on the river Donau. There he died on the Day of Damascus, the anniversary of St. Paul's first mystical vision of the Risen Christ, January 25, 1366, at the age of seventy-one.

Through the Dominican stream the Scholasticism of Thomas Aquinas came to Meister Eckhart in the form of ideas which he shaped and fashioned into aphoristic expression by means of his remarkable powers of thinking; in the hands of Johannes Tauler Scholasticism was transformed into Christian action, into practical deeds of will; in the golden warmth of his loving, devoted heart Heinrich Suso bathed Scholasticism in a lyric splendor of poetic imagery so that it became a thing of transcendent, eternal beauty.

4

Jan van Ruysbroeck was born in the little village of Ruysbroeck on the Senne between Brussels and Hal in 1293, the year after the death of the English Franciscan philosopher and scientist, Roger Bacon. When Jan was eleven years old he decided to run away from home in order that he might more completely dedicate himself and his life to God. He went to the house of his uncle, Jan Hinckaert in Brussels, and asked if the latter would undertake to educate him to the service of God. The uncle, who was a Canon of the Church of Saint Gudale in Brussels, arranged that the boy would live in his home and study with his friend, the learned priest, Franc van Coudenberg, and himself. Eventually Jan took the four-year course in the Latin School of Brussels, and from there he attended the well-known theological school in Cologne.

At the age of twenty-four Jan van Ruysbroeck was ordained a priest, and was appointed chaplain to his uncle in Brussels. His life for the next two decades seems to have been that of a dedicated pastor, who served his congregation to the best of his ability, but was not otherwise particularly distinguished, at least externally.

However, as Jan van Ruysbroeck's fiftieth birthday approached, he had a remarkable experience. He felt that the time had come when he was to withdraw from further work in the world, and that he was called to devote himself entirely to spiritual matters. At about the same time his uncle was deeply confused and depressed one day, and an inner voice directed him to go into the church. As he did so, he saw that a visiting missionary priest had just mounted the pulpit to preach to the congregation. Now the uncle knew that this priest had a serious speech defect. To the uncle's astonishment, as the missionary opened his mouth, the words flowed out in a river of eloquence. At this, the preacher turned to where the uncle was standing and said, "This miracle has happened for the sake of that man standing there, in order that he will repent and turn to God."

In similar manner, van Coudenberg also had a spiritual experience, and was filled with the deep desire to live a more dedicated life.

At Easter 1343, the three men resigned their work in Brussels and went deep into the forest of Soignes where they found a deserted hunting-lodge called the Green Valley (*Grönendal*). The place had not been used for over a generation, and the men set to work to make a home for themselves there, and soon had built a chapel. Others joined them, and before long a small community had developed.

After about six years the community decided to take on the rule and habit of the Augustinian canons. And the moving spirit was Jan van Ruysbroeck himself, who was as devoted to practical tasks as he was to spiritual matters. Whether it was necessary to repair a stove, load a manure cart, discuss deep problems of theology, or nurse the sick, he was always ready and cheerfully willing to do whatever was to be done.

The fame of the little forest community spread, and visitors came from far places to see the life that was being lived there. One day two young priests, theological students from the University of Paris, arrived and asked to speak with Jan van Ruysbroeck. They wished his advice concerning their spiritual development, and begged that he would help them to find the way to the spirit, and would speak with them about the condition of their souls. His reply was to the point: "You are as spiritual as you have the desire to be, that is all." They were somewhat annoyed at the abruptness of his words, and turned away. At once he spoke to them in a loving tone: "My very dear children, I said your spirituality was what you wish it to be so that you would understand that your spirituality is entirely in proportion to your good will. Then enter into yourselves; don't ask others about your progress. Examine your good will, and from that alone you will discover the measure of your spirituality."

One of the guests at Grönendal was Johannes Tauler, who was much impressed with the life he saw there. In turn, Tauler doubtless told Jan van Ruysbroeck about his experiences with the Friends of God.

In 1378, the year after Gregory XI condemned John Wycliffe, translator of the Vulgate into English as a heretic, the famous lay-preacher Gerard Groote visited the community of Grönendal and had many conversations with Jan van Ruysbroeck.

Gerard Groote was born in the town of Deventer, about sixty miles from Amsterdam in 1340. His parents were wealthy, and at the age of fifteen Gerard was sent to the University of Paris. In three years he was given his Master's degree, and then was called to teach at Cologne, where he was soon advanced to the position of professor of philosophy, and also received important appointments of a civil nature.

One day Groote was standing with a crowd watching a game in a Cologne square when a modestly dressed stranger, with a serious, sincere face approached him and spoke to him softly: "Why are you standing here? You ought to become *another man*." Soon after this incident Groote fell seriously ill, and his life was despaired of. However, when matters were at their worst, he recalled the words of the stranger, and at once promised Heaven that he would do everything in his power to become "another man" if he was allowed to regain his health. Groote recovered, and not long after was sought out by his former teacher from the University of Paris, Henry de Kalkar, who for some years had been the prior of a Carthusian monastery near Deventer. This dedicated man had come to Groote, impelled by an inner urge to call the latter to a new life.

Groote retired from the world, and dedicated himself to the pursuit of spiritual things. Eventually the time came when his studies entitled him to be ordained a priest. This he refused, and refused repeatedly to the end of his life.

In 1379 Groote sensed a spiritual call to go out into the countryside as an itinerant lay-preacher. The Bishop of Utrecht granted him a license as a preacher, allowing him to speak anywhere in his diocese.

According to all accounts Groote was a speaker of marked excellence. He differed radically from other preachers of his time in that he never threatened his hearers with punishments of hell nor sought to bribe them with the bliss of heaven. He spoke simply and directly to them of the love of God, the great way of salvation, the search for the good, and always about the wonderful possibilities of a life lived in consonance with God. He spoke only from his personal experience, never used any Latin phrases in his discourses, and employed only the simplest, most direct forms of expression. The result was that for five years people flocked to hear him wherever he went.

In the course of his wanderings Groote visited Grönendal and was deeply impressed by everything he saw, most of all by the entirely practical attitude toward life which Jan van Ruysbroeck manifested. From that Groote was inspired to form a community, a kind of Christian brotherhood, which would be bound by no permanent vows as were monks, but would consist of individuals who freely chose to live together in poverty, chastity, obedience, simplicity, and piety, holding all possessions in common as the early Christians had done, and working together to earn their own livelihood.

Groote was soon surrounded by a group of men who enthusiastically wished to take up this life, and who took the name "Brotherhood of the Common Lot" or the "Common Life." The first community house was established at Deventer, and was called a "brother house." Soon "sister houses" for women were also established. Groote loved books, and therefore he freely gave his fortune for the purchase of rare books, which the brothers and sisters copied by hand—this, of course, was before the invention of the printing press. The money received from the sale of these volumes was used for the maintenance of the communities. The Brothers and Sisters of the Common Life mingled freely with the world, and soon came to be recognized everywhere in Holland, Belgium and in the German Rhine valley by their plain grey habit and their simple, unassuming manners. Their life was devoted to the care of orphan children, the spreading of knowledge through the sale of books that they copied, and in the teaching of reading and writing to adults. Their method of instruction of children was based on practical life, and was directed toward moral and spiritual improvement. They taught the children under their care to earn a living, but never encouraged them to enter a profession which would give them undue wealth.

Jan van Ruysbroeck's last days were spent quietly in the community at Grönendal, and many stories were told of his remarkable spiritual development. For example, he was missing one day, and at last was found sitting beneath a tree in the forest, sunk in deep meditation, while, according to the tale, the tree itself was surrounded by a heavenly brightness of shimmering colors.

He knew the force of directness in conversation. A man once tried to draw him out on the subject of the dreadful wickedness in the world. His only remark was, "What we are, that we behold; and what we behold, that we are."

Like many mystics, he loved animals and flowers, and his greatest earthly joy was in the song of the birds of the forest. His death took place in 1381, the year of the outbreak of the Peasant Revolt in England under the leadership of Wat Tyler and the priest John Ball. Stories tell how at the moment of his death, the bells of the churches in neighboring villages began to toll all by themselves, and how after several years when his corpse was exhumed it showed no decomposition, but gave off a sweet odor which healed the sick who were brought near.

Gerhart Groote survived Jan van Ruysbroeck by three years. Meanwhile, a young man had joined the circle of the Brotherhood of the Common Life who is known as the author of one of the most important books of devotion in the world. His name was Thomas à Kempis, and his *Imitation of Christ* is a classic which has inspired many people throughout the centuries since it first appeared. Thomas also was the biographer of Gerhard Groote, and his impression of the Brotherhood of the Common Life was, "I never before recall having seen men so devout, so full of love for God and their fellow-men. Living in the world, they were altogether unworldly."

At the conclusion of Thomas' life of Gerhard Groote is a collection of aphorisms which he attributes to the latter as among the basic teachings of the Brotherhood of the Common Life: "Conquer yourself. Turn your heart from things, and direct your mind continually to God. Do not for any cause allow yourself to lose your composure. Practice obedience, and accept things that are difficult. Continually exercise yourself in humility and moderation. The further one knows himself to be from perfection, the closer he is to it. Of all temptations, the greatest is not to be tempted at all. Never breathe so much as a word to display your religion or learning. Nothing is a better test of a man than to hear himself praised. Above all, and first of all, let Christ be the basis of your study and the mirror of your life."

Years after the deaths of Jan van Ruysbroeck and Gerhard Groote, a twelve-year-old boy was brought to the Brethren of the Common Life at Deventer, and was placed in the school there. Destined to be one of the most important figures of the Reformation period, Desiderius Erasmus, became famous for his modesty, his temperance and wisdom. These qualities are no doubt traceable to the early training he received at the hands of the Brethren of the Common Life. Erasmus of Rotterdam advised moderation and tolerance, even when the opposite qualities ran high, as for example in his famous letter in reply to the Pope's invitation to come to Rome in order to advise him on how to deal with Luther and his followers: "You ask me what you should do. Some believe there is no remedy but force. I do not believe this, for I think there would be dreadful bloodshed.... If you intend to try prison, lash, stake and scaffold, you do not need my help...."

About the Author, the People, and the Background 161

Discover the roots of the disease and clean them out first of all. Punish nobody, but let what has happened be considered as a visitation of Providence, and extend a general amnesty to all." Had the moderation counselled in this letter, typical of the spirit of the Brotherhood of the Common Life, been followed, how different might the course of history have been!

5

In 1401, when Ghiberti's Baptistry doors, "worthy to be the gates of Paradise," were first shown to the admiring eyes of his fellow Florentines, and the English Parliament decreed that all proven heretics were to be burned at the stake, Nicholas Chrypfls was born at Cusa on the Moselle River. Nicholas was to be known as "the last great philosopher of the dying Middle Ages," and was to fling wide the doors of those medieval minds to the concept of a universe that is infinite. As a student he made a brilliant record in his study of law and mathematics at the renowned University of Padua, and followed this with a course in theology at Cologne where, as we have seen, he was preceded by Meister Eckhart, Tauler, Suso, van Ruysbroeck, and Groote. Eventually Nicholas became Archdeacon of Liège at about the time that Joan of Arc was burned at the stake in Rouen.

The Council of Basel, which had convened intermittently since 1417, was beginning its last ten years of existence when Nicholas attended its sessions in his official capacity as Archdeacon of Liège in 1437. These sessions took place at the time when Cosimo de Medici was making preparations for the opening of his famous Platonic Academy in Florence, the institution renowned as a center of revival of the learning of the classical world.

Shortly after his attendance at the Council of Basel, Nicholas was sent to Constantinople to try his efforts toward the solution of one of the most vexing problems of the time, the reunion of the churches of East and West. His work at Basel and Constantinople attracted the attention of the Pope, so that in 1440 Nicholas was sent to Germany as papal legate at a very critical moment in the relations between Germany and the Church of Rome.

When Nicholas arrived in Germany, Frederick, Duke of Styria was chosen king to rule as Frederick IV. Just at that time the Council of Basel had appointed an "anti-pope," called Felix V, in opposition to Pope Eugenius IV. In the fact that soon after his election, Frederick decided to extend his influence to the support of Eugenius in opposition to the Council of Basel, one perhaps can see the fruit of the work of Nicholas of Cusa as papal legate in Germany.

It also seems something more than coincidence that in 1448, when Frederick IV and Pope Nicolas V signed the Concordat of Vienna, by which the German church was firmly rebound to Rome, Nicholas of Cusa was raised to the rank of Cardinal. Two years later he was appointed Bishop of Britten.

The reactionary character of the Concordat of Vienna made impossible any reform of conditions within the German church. The clergy in Germany who had hoped for some easing of the repressive measures of the papacy, were doomed to disappointment. On the other hand, the Concordat of Vienna was one of the principal links in the chain of events that finally culminated on All Saints' Day, 1517, when Martin Luther nailed his theses to the door of the church in Wittenberg, and the German Reformation became a fact.

The sixteen years (1448–1464) of the Cardinalate of Nicholas of Cusa coincide with remarkable developments in the social and cultural life of the Western world. The year 1452 is notable as the year of the birth of two men of marked divergence of outlook. The first was Girolamo Savonarola, the Dominican monk, leader of the reaction against the Renaissance, the dogmatic eschatologist from Ferrara, who as "dictator of Florence" held a brief sway over the minds and bodies of the people of his time. Also in 1452 was born the genius of the Renaissance, the archetype of the "new man," the very incarnation of the spirit of progress, of universality, of investigation, of freedom from traditionalism and conservatism—Leonardo da Vinci. At this same time a host of the world's most famous Greek scholars left Constantinople in fear of the advancing Turks under Mohammed II, who finally took the city the following year, which also marked the end of the Hundred Years' War in Western Europe.

In 1454, as a kind of picture of things to come in the field of technical development and invention, Johannes Gutenberg issued his first texts printed with movable type, and before two more years were completed, published his edition of the Vulgate Bible at Mainz. 1456 is notable as the year the Turks captured Athens and subsequently all Greece, thus marking the end of the last vestiges of classicism remaining in that country.

Pica della Mirandola, famous Renaissance scholar and writer, collector of precious books and manuscripts, master of Greek, Latin, Hebrew, Chaldee and Arabic, student of the mysticism of the Kabbalah and other mystical writings, was born in 1463. The following year, on August 11, Nicholas of Cusa died, renowned as a distinguished prince of the Church, and as a diplomat traveling in the service of the Pope.

Today Nicholas of Cusa is remembered for his cosmological conceptions, his originality and breadth of thought, and his courage as a thinker at a time when the rationalized dogmatic system of Scholasticism was breaking down in face of the impact of the new age. As the famous French mathematician and philosopher, René Descartes was to write nearly two hundred years after Nicholas' death, "The Cardinal of Cusa and several other theologians have supposed the world to be infinite, and the Church has never condemned them for it. On the contrary, it is thought that to make His works appear very great is one way to honor God." Nicholas of Cusa's work was appreciated by such men as Giordano Bruno, philosopher;, poet, and martyr; Johannes Kepler, the astronomer; and Descartes, to name but a few. The courage necessary for a thinker to grasp the implications of the new age was present in Nicholas of Cusa, and the scope of his investigations in the world of thought is evidence of his importance and stature.

6

The year 1487 is regarded by some as the year of the beginning of the Renaissance. By others it is remembered as the time the Portuguese navigator, Bartholomew Diaz, sailing along the African coast on a voyage of exploration, discovered the Cape of Good Hope and thereby opened the passage to India and China. Still others recall that this was the year of the birth of one Henry Cornelius, generally known as Agrippa of Nettesheim, in the city of Cologne on September 14. His family was honored for its service to the royal house of Hapsburg, but little is known of his childhood and youth.

Like others whom we have considered, Henry Cornelius studied at the University of Cologne. While still a young man, he learned eight languages and passed some time in France.

In 1486, the year before Henry Cornelius was born, the son of Frederick IV, whom Nicholas of Cusa had supported in signing the Concordat of Vienna, came to the throne of Germany as Maximilian I. The latter was heir to great areas of Austria, and was administrator of the Netherlands. Not long after he came to the throne of Germany he united the country, and through the marriage of his son Philip to the heiress of the Spanish kingdoms, his influence soon spread to that country as well. Thus Maximilian exercised a power in Europe as had no German ruler for centuries.

While he was still a young man, Henry Cornelius was appointed secretary in the service of Maximilian, and his life of travel and adventure began almost at once. However, the life of the battlefield and the court did not suit him, and not long afterward we find him at the University of Dole as a lecturer on philosophy. This appointment was made in 1509, the year that Erasmus wrote his *Chiliades adagiorum*, by which his reputation as an author was established.

But Henry Cornelius' lectures did not long escape the attention of the Inquisition, and it became necessary for him to go to England on a diplomatic mission for Maximilian as the result of an attack made upon him by the monk John Catilinet who was lecturing at Ghent. In London Henry Cornelius was a welcome guest in the home of Dr. John Colet—who was friend and later the patron of Erasmus, student of the teachings of Savonarola, former lecturer at Oxford, and at that time dean of St. Paul's Cathedral. In his later life, Colet was to preach on the occasion of Wolsey's installation as cardinal, and was to become chaplain to Henry VIII. He did much to introduce the humanist teachings of the Renaissance into England, and was an outspoken opponent of auricular confession and the celibacy of the clergy of the Catholic Church.

After his return to the Continent, Henry Cornelius went to Italy with Maximilian on one of the latter's expeditions against Venice. During his stay in Italy in 1512—the year the Medici were recalled to Florence, and Martin Luther was made a Doctor of Theology—he attended the Council of Pisa as a theologian. This council had been called by a group of Cardinals in opposition to militaristic plans of Pope Julius II who had laid the cornerstone for the new basilica of St. Peter's in Rome six years before.

In all, Henry Cornelius remained in Italy about seven years, and they were a very eventful time, for they coincided with some of the most important events of the Renaissance period. In these years the Aldine edition of Plato's work appeared in Venice; Niccolo Machiavelli wrote *The Prince,* a landmark in the history of political thought; and Erasmus published his New Testament in Greek. Julius II died during this period; and Giovanni de Medici, made Cardinal at fourteen, now became Pope Leo X. His famous exclamation, "Since God has given us the papacy, let us enjoy it," set a pattern for the Renaissance, while his permission to sell indulgences for the benefit of the construction of St. Peter's led to the upheaval of the Reformation.

Henry Cornelius was active as a physician during his first years in Italy, first in the household of the Marquis of Monferrato, later in that of the Duke of Savoy. In 1515 he accepted an invitation to lecture at the University of Pavia on one of the works of the ancient world beloved by the adherents of the new learning of the

Renaissance, the *Pimander* of Hermes Trismegistus. This was the year when Sir Thomas More wrote his *Utopia,* and Leonardo da Vinci left Rome for the last time enroute to his three-year exile and death in France.

The university lectures on the *Pimander* were suddenly broken off as a result of the victorious advance into Italy by the armies of Francis I of France. Henry Cornelius returned to Germany, and in 1518, the year Zwingli began the Reformation among the Swiss, he was appointed town advocate of Metz. But he was not left in peace for long. First, the death of Maximilian at the beginning of 1519 and the subsequent election of Charles V—King of Spain, Naples, Sicily, ruler of the Netherlands, Austria, Burgundy, and of dominions in the New World—as ruler of Germany brought changes in the life of Henry Cornelius. Second, a woman was tried in Metz for witchcraft. In his position as town advocate Henry Cornelius went to her defense, with the result that he became involved in a serious controversy with one of the most dreaded agents of the Inquisition, the notorious Nicholas Savin. Finally, in 1520, the year of Magellan's voyage around the world, of the death of the painter Raphael, and of Luther's burning of the papal bull, Henry Cornelius quietly left Metz for Cologne, where he remained in discreet retirement for about two years.

He appeared in public life again, first in Geneva, afterward in Freiburg, where he practiced as a physician. In 1524, a year before Tyndale's English translation of the New Testament appeared, he went to Lyons to accept a post as physician to Louise of Savoy, mother of Francis I. But the unsettled times—now accentuated by the terrible sack of Rome by the armies of Constable Bourbon in 1517—caused him to relinquish the position in favor of some post further north which might offer greater security for his study and work.

That Henry Cornelius was considered an able scholar is evidenced by the fact that at about this time he was offered the opportunity to participate in a disputation concerning the legality of the divorce action between Henry VIII of England and Catharine of

Aragon, which was then taking place. However, he accepted an offer to be archivist and historian to Charles V, which Louise of Savoy obtained for him.

The death of Louise of Savoy in 1531 weakened his position, and in addition to all of the other ferment of the time, the news that Henry VIII had declared himself "Supreme Head of the Church of England" only increased the uncertainty of conditions. Also, Henry Cornelius had published several works which had attracted the attention of the Inquisition, and for a time he was imprisoned in Brussels. However, despite the publication of his *Concerning Secret Science (De occulta philosophia)*—written about 1510 and printed in Antwerp in 1531—which the Inquisition did their best to prevent, Henry Cornelius was able to live for some time at Cologne and Bonn under the personal protection of the great Hermann van Wied, Archbishop of Cologne, who recognized and appreciated his remarkable qualities as a scholar and man.

At the very end of his life, while he was visiting Paris, Francis I had him arrested on the strength of a report that he had spoken badly of the reputation of the queen mother. The charge was proven false, and he was released after a brief imprisonment; but the strain of the experience was too great for him to bear, and he died suddenly at Grenoble on February 18, 1535, at the age of forty-nine. His death took place in the same year as that of Sir Thomas More, and five years after that of Erasmus.

Henry Cornelius was married three times, and was the father of a large family of children. Despite attacks by the Inquisition on his reputation and teachings that went on long after his death—his memory has been kept alive through the years because of his writings, mainly his *Concerning Secret Science*. A man of unusual courage and in some ways a kind of universal genius, Henry Cornelius was typical of the men whose lives spanned the period that opened the way to the modern age.

7

Columbus had reached America on his western voyage; Lorenzo de Medici had died in Florence; the Spaniard Rodrigo Borgia, along with his mistress and children, now inhabited the Vatican as Pope Alexander VI, whose frankly pagan orgies were more fitting to the later Roman emperors than to the Vicar of Christ upon earth; and in the little Swiss town of Einsiedeln in Canton Schwyz, the local physician, illegitimate son of a Grand Master of the Teutonic Order, was in turn the father of a son whom he named Theophrastus Bombast van Hohenheim. Later, the son himself chose the name by which he is known to history—Paracelsus.

The boy's early education was in the hands of his father; at the age of sixteen he entered the University of Basel. However, his restless nature and his independent thinking made formal study most unattractive to him, and he determined to seek an education in his own way.

About this time he heard of the great Benedictine scholar, Johannes Trithemius, originally Abbot of the Monastery of Wurzburg, later of Sponheim near Kreuznach. The Abbot of Sponheim was celebrated for the remarkable library he had collected, for his studies in cryptography, for his writings on history, and for his researches in alchemy and related sciences. This same Abbot of Sponheim had greatly influenced Henry Cornelius in the latter's work on his *Concerning Secret Science.*

Paracelsus decided to apply to the Abbot of Sponheim for the opportunity to study science with him. He was accepted, but the association did not last very long. Led by a desire to learn more about the nature and properties of minerals first-hand, he went to the Tyrolean mines owned by the famous merchant-administrators and bankers to the German Emperors, the Fuggers.

Paracelsus felt at home among the miners. He soon came to the conviction that what he gained through direct observation was the best education of all. He learned about the processes involved in mining operations, the nature of ores, the properties of mineral waters, and the stratification of the rocks of the earth. Meanwhile he came to know the home life of the miners, studied their illnesses and the types of accidents to which they were most prone. In brief, from his experiences in the mines he concluded that formal schooling is not education in the mysteries of nature. He was convinced that only by reading the book of nature first-hand and through personal contact with those who work with nature can one come to anything like truly natural scientific knowledge.

This point of view followed Paracelsus throughout his life, and colored his relationships with those scholars with whom he came into contact. He based his work entirely on the results of his own observation and experience, and not on theories acquired from others.

Paracelsus wandered over a great part of central Europe in order that he might come to a direct personal knowledge of things. He once said that the physician must read the book of nature, and that to do so he must "walk over its pages." He came to the conclusion that since the temperaments, constitutions and activities of different peoples are different, the diseases from which they suffer must also be different. Therefore he believed that it was incumbent upon the physician to know other peoples as the key to understanding his own.

The summation of Paracelsus' method of study is contained in his questions, "From where do I obtain all my secrets, from what authors? It would be better if one asked how the animals have learned their skills. If nature can teach irrational animals, can it not much more teach human beings?"

In all, Paracelsus spent nearly a full decade in his wanderings in search of knowledge. At the end of his travels, while the mass of information he had gathered lacked order and coherence, there is no doubt that here was a man whose experiences, observations of peoples, places and events, as well as knowledge of the elements and processes of nature gave his words and deeds the weight of direct evidence. His superiority to his contemporaries was unquestionable.

When Paracelsus returned to Basel in 1527 he was appointed city physician, and also was made professor of physic, medicine, and surgery at the University. He undertook to give a course of lectures in medicine, but the latter provoked a storm of protest because they were so unconventional, as might have been expected from one holding his views on education. First of all, Paracelsus lectured in German, not Latin, which was unheard of in academic circles of the time. Then, his lectures were composed of statements derived from his experience and presented his own methods of cure, based upon his personal points of view. But worst of all to the traditionalists, Paracelsus' lectures dealt with the cure of the diseases current among the peoples of Europe in the year 1527, and not only did they not include comment on the classic medical texts of Galen or Avicenna (Ibn Sina)—an accepted part of every medical lecture worthy of the name—but they attacked these sacrosanct authorities and ridiculed those who followed their teachings. Above all, Paracelsus pleaded for a medical practice that met the needs of the time, that followed the results of direct observation, and that did away with the ignorance and greed of physicians hiding behind a mask of pompousness and reliance upon the dicta of men who had been dead for centuries.

Paracelsus also was hard at work proving the practical worth of his knowledge in curing the sick. His success was phenomenal. Maladies previously considered incurable were healed quickly and efficiently by his methods. Case after case that had been given up by other physicians of Basel and the surrounding towns, was brought to him and cured. For two or three years Paracelsus' reputation spread far and wide. Never before had such a physician practiced in Basel!

But this success did not last. At first, his learning, derived from his practical experience, his appeal to the common sense of his hearers, captured the imagination of his students. His successful practice was proof of the correctness of his teaching, and all opposition based on traditionalism was pushed aside.

Slowly, however, the tide began to turn; the waters of opposition gathered their strength. No single detail escaped the vigilant eyes of his enemies; nothing was too insignificant to throw into the scale against him. There was the matter of his not having a degree; the conservatives demanded that he be forced to prove his qualifications before continuing his teaching and practice. And his prescriptions were a source of annoyance to the pharmacists of Basel, for Paracelsus had worked out his own system of drug compounding, which differed radically from that generally employed by other physicians. Therefore, the apothecaries attacked Paracelsus because he did not use their products as did the Galenists. On the other hand, Paracelsus requested the city authorities to keep close watch on the purity of the drugs sold in Basel, to be certain that the apothecaries really knew their work, and, above all, to be watchful of the commercial relationships between the apothecaries and physicians.

At last the day came for which the enemies of Paracelsus had long been waiting. Among his patients was one Canon Cornelius von Lichtenfels who had called upon Paracelsus for professional aid when his own physician had given up his case. Although he had promised to pay Paracelsus' fee in the event of a cure, von Lichtenfels now refused to do so. Eventually the matter was taken into a court of law, where the judges found in favor of von Lichtenfels. Noted for his quickness of temper and outspokenness, Paracelsus candidly told the judges his opinion of them, their conduct of the case, and their method of administering the law. When he left the court, Paracelsus' friends advised him to leave Basel without delay, for his enemies would surely see to it that he be severely punished for his speech before the justices. Paracelsus took this advice, and departed from Basel in haste.

Once again Paracelsus resumed his wandering life. For a brief time he remained in Esslingen, then went to Colmar, but the pinch of poverty drove him from town to town in search of work. Twelve years were passed in these journeyings, Paracelsus never remaining in one place for more than a year.

Finally, in 1541, when Paracelsus was forty-eight, he received an invitation which seemed to be the fulfillment of his longing for a permanent home where he could pursue his work undisturbed and in peace. Archbishop Ernst of Salzburg offered Paracelsus his protection if the latter would come to that city and take up his professional activities there.

But Paracelsus was in Salzburg only a few months when he died at almost the same time Michelangelo completed his painting of the "Last Judgment" in the Sistine Chapel at Rome.

Even the reports of Paracelsus' death reflect the efforts of his enemies to defame him. One tale recounts that his death was caused by a drunken brawl in which he was a participant. A report with sinister implications tells that Paracelsus did not die a natural death, but was thrown over a steep cliff at night by assassins in the employ of the apothecaries and physicians, whose vengeance followed him through all his years of exile.

One of Paracelsus' most far-reaching concepts is that of Signatures, that is, the idea that each single part of the microcosmic world of the human being corresponds with each single part of the macrocosmic world. This leads directly to his teaching concerning Specifics. He realized that the latter were not to be discovered in the labyrinth of often fantastic nostrums and combinations of substances prescribed in the writings of the Galenists. Through careful observation extending over many years, Paracelsus concluded that mineral, plant and animal substances contain within themselves what he called "active principles." It was his conviction that if a method of purification and intensification could be discovered whereby these substances could be caused to release their "active principles," the latter would be infinitely more efficacious and safer in producing a cure than would their crude and often dangerous originals.

Paracelsus died before he could discover the method that could unlock the potency—the healing power latent in mineral, plant and animal substances. This problem was not solved until two and a half centuries later when another physician, Samuel Hahnemann, discovered a method of so handling mineral, plant and animal substances that their innate healing powers were enhanced and made available to a medical practice in line with the highest ideals of cure envisioned by Paracelsus. This method of preparation of substances and the manner of their selection and administration to the sick, Hahnemann called Homeopathy.

The first of Paracelsus' extensive works was published in Augsburg in 1529, memorable as the year when the Reformers' presentation of a protest to the Diet of Spires won them the name of Protestants. Throughout the extensive writings of Paracelsus, repeated again and again in every one of the more than two hundred separate publications of his works that appeared between 1542 and 1845, a single theme is to be observed: The life of human beings cannot be separated from the life of the universe; therefore, to understand human beings, understand the universe; to understand the universe, understand human beings. Only upon such an understanding—universal in its scope—Paracelsus believed a medical art worthy of the name could be built. To the proclamation of such a goal of medicine he devoted his life.

In one of his writings, Paracelsus says, "There is a light in the human spirit... by which the qualities of each thing created by God, whether it be visible or invisible to the senses, may be perceived and known. If we knows the essence of things, their attributes, their attractions, and the elements of which they consist, we will be a master of nature, of the elements, and of the spirits."

Robert Browning expressed these thoughts in the well-known lines:

> Truth is within ourselves; it takes no rise
> From outward things, what'er you may believe.
> There is an inmost center in us all,
> Where truth abides in fulness; and around,
> Wall upon wall, the gross flesh hems it in,
> This perfect, clear perception—which is truth,
> A baffling and perverting carnal mesh
> Binds it, and makes all error: and, to KNOW,
> Rather consists in opening out a way
> Whence the imprisoned splendor may escape,
> Than in effecting entry for a light
> Supposed to be without.

8

Eight years before the death of Paracelsus, Valentine Weigel was born at Naundorff, near Grossenheim in the district of Meissen. This year 1533 was also the year of the birth of Montaigne, the skeptic, of the completion of the rape of Peru by the most notorious of all Spanish conquistadores, Francisco Pizarro, of the proclamation of Anne Boleyn, soon to be the mother of Elizabeth, as Queen of England by Henry VIII, and of the final preparation of Luther's complete German Bible which was published the next year.

The details of Weigel's childhood are obscure, but in course of time he received his bachelor's and master's degrees at the University of Leipzig. He continued his studies at the University of Wittenberg until 1567, three years after the death of Michelangelo. In that year he was ordained a Lutheran pastor and was called to the church at Zschopau, not far from Chemnitz in eastern Germany. His life was passed entirely in this place, and he continued as pastor of this church until his death in 1588, the year the English defeated the Spanish Armada.

While the external events of Weigel's life are few and somewhat unimpressive when compared with some of the biographies discussed thus far, his inner development and his dedication to his pastoral tasks are very remarkable. He is remembered as a loving, devoted man, a true shepherd of his flock, a man whom all his parishioners loved, and who loved them in return. Twenty-one years after the death of their pastor, his parishioners came to know that in addition to this Valentin Weigel that they knew, another man, as it were, had been active all the years in Zschopau. This was Valentin Weigel, student, mystic, and author.

Weigel had long been a close student of the writings of Paracelsus, whose work he deeply admired, but whose fate he was determined not to share. Therefore, while he studied and wrote a great deal during his lifetime, he never revealed his interest in mysticism to anyone, and left instructions that his writings were not to be published until sometime after his death. So while Pastor Weigel stood in his pulpit and preached to his flock Sunday after Sunday without interruption for twenty-one years, he never shared his most cherished interests and convictions with them.

Weigel was well acquainted with the works of Eckhart and Tauler and also with such classical mystics as Dionysius and the neo-Platonists. With all his study, he recognized that the ultimate truth of things is not acquired from without, but is to be found within each person. He wrote, "Study nature, physics, alchemy, magic, and so on, but *it is all in you*, and you become what you have learned."

In 1609, the year Henry Hudson sailed up the river that now bears his name, twenty-one years after Weigel's death, his book, which was to greatly influence English mystics after its translation into English in 1648, was published. It bore the title *Of the Life of Christ, that is, of True Faith* (*Con den Leben Christi, das ist, vom wahren Glauben*). One of its outstanding passages is, "Faith comes by inward hearing. Good books, external preaching, have their place; they testify to the real Treasure. They are witnesses to the Word within us. But faith is not tied to books; Faith is a *new birth*, which cannot be found in books. The one who has the inner Schoolmaster would lose nothing of his salvation, even though all the preachers should die and all books be burned."

Considering the theological ideas prevailing in his time, one of Weigel's most interesting concepts deals with the location of heaven and hell. In an age when basically materialistic descriptions of heavenly wonders were contrasted with equally materialistic portrayals of hellish tortures, and people were assured by their pastors that these were definite *places*, Weigel's conviction, which probably he never voiced from his pulpit, is surprisingly modern. He wrote that "Heaven and Hell are in the soul of man, after all; both Trees of Paradise, the Tree of Knowledge of Good and Evil, as well as the Tree of Life, flourish in the human soul" (See Weigel's *Know Thyself*).

Like Luther and others, Weigel prized and edited the little book, *Theologia Germanica*, or *The Golden Book of German Theology*, as

Henry More called it, and spoke of it as "a precious little book, a noble book." Weigel also loved the sermons of Johannes Tauler because "they testify to the experience of the Heavenly Jerusalem within us."

For Weigel, the immanence of the spiritual world was a profound conviction, born of his personal experience. His expression of this is one of the classic statements of mysticism: "God is nearer to us than we are to ourselves."

9

Jacob Boehme was born on April 24, 1575, in the little German village of Alt Seidenberg on a hillside south of Goerlitz, near the Bohemian border. Jacob was the fourth child of his parents, of old German peasant stock, noted for their honesty and devoutness. The Boehme family were staunch Lutherans, and the children were brought up according to the family faith. Jacob was a sickly child, and was not thought strong enough to work in the fields. Therefore, his childhood summers were spent watching the herds, and in winter he received the rudiments of reading, writing, simple arithmetic and a little Latin. His favorite reading was his Bible, which he carried with him in the fields, and came to know as few other men have.

When he was fourteen, his father apprenticed him to the village cobbler for three years, since it was clear that Jacob's health would never permit him to be a farmer. In 1592 Jacob Boehme began his journeyman's wanderings.

Abraham von Franckenberg, whom we shall meet again as the friend of Johannes Scheffler (Angelus Silesius), knew Jacob Boehme, and described the latter's appearance in these years: "Jacob's body was worn and plain. He was short, with low forehead, wide temples, his nose slightly crooked, and his grey eyes lighting up at times like the windows of Solomon's Temple. He had a short beard, somewhat thin, and a slight voice, which was very gentle in conversation. His manner was modest, mild and humble. He was of patient heart, and his spirit was lightened by God beyond anything to be found in nature."

In the chapter in this book dealing with Jacob Boehme, Rudolf Steiner relates the famous story of the stranger and the pair of shoes, which took place during Boehme's apprentice days, sometime before 1599. In May of that year Boehme was officially made a citizen of Goerlitz, became established as a master shoemaker there, and soon afterward married Catherina Kuntzsch, daughter of a butcher of Goerlitz, by whom he had four children.

In the year 1600, when Jacob Boehme was twenty-five, he had the remarkable spiritual experience that Rudolf Steiner mentions in this book. Boehme saw the sunlight reflected on the surface of a polished pewter dish, and it was suddenly as though he could penetrate into the most secret depths of the universe, could probe the secrets of nature, and could fathom the essential being of everything in creation. This is comparable to Paracelsus' observation: "Hidden things which cannot be perceived by the physical senses may be discovered by means of the sidereal body, through whose organism we can look into nature just as the sun shines through a glass."

Boehme later explained his spiritual experience or "illumination" in the introduction to his book, *Aurora:* "In a quarter of an hour, I observed and knew more than if I had attended a university for many years. I recognized the Being of Beings, both the Byss and Abyss, the eternal generation of the Trinity, the origin and creation of this world and of all creatures through the Divine Wisdom. I saw all three worlds in myself: first, the Divine World; second, the dark world and the source of fire; third, the external, visible world as an outbreathing of the inner or spiritual worlds. I also saw the fundamental nature of evil and good, and how the pregnant Mother, the eternal genetrix, brought them forth. My experience is like the evoking of life in the presence of death, or like the resurrection from the dead. My spirit suddenly saw all created things, even the herbs and grass, in this light. I knew who God is, what He is like, and the nature of His Will. Suddenly in that light my will was seized by a mighty impulse to describe the Being of God." For ten long years after this spiritual experience, to which Boehme referred repeatedly throughout the remainder of his life, he meditated on his vision. He came to believe that what he had to tell others was entirely unique with him, and that his mission was to purify Christianity, which he thought had become corrupt once again. He had no use for theology born of reason, nor for creeds and dogmas established on purely intellectual foundations. He was convinced that only one's personal experience of the reality of the spiritual world can enable one to overcome evil and advance into genuine knowledge of the spirit.

In 1610, the year when Galileo discovered the satellites of Jupiter by means of the newly-invented telescope, Jacob Boehme knew that the moment had come when he could write down an account of what he had seen a decade before: "To write these things was strongly urged upon my spirit, however difficult they might be for my outer self to understand, and for my pen to express. Like a child beginning school I was compelled to start my work on this very great Mystery. Within myself I saw it well enough, as in a great depth, but the describing and explaining of it seemed impossible."

Boehme wrote in the early morning before he went to his cobbler's bench, and in the evening after he returned home from his work. And at last, after two years of diligent effort, Jacob Boehme produced his *Aurora,* one of the masterpieces of mystical literature.

That Boehme knew that the twenty-six chapters of his *Aurora* are not easy to read, and are not for everyman, is clear from his words: "If you are not a spiritual overcomer, then let my book alone. Don't meddle with it, but stick to your old ways.... Art was not written here, nor did I find time to consider how to set things down accurately, according to rules of composition, but everything followed the direction of the Spirit, which often hastened so that the writer's hand shook. As the burning fire of the Spirit hurried ahead, the hand and pen had to follow after it, for it came and went like a sudden shower."

Handwritten copies of the manuscript were made by Carl Ender von Sercha, Boehme's friend and student. Sercha believed that in Boehme's work a prophecy of Paracelsus had been fulfilled, which announced that the years between 1599 and 1603 would bring about a new age for humankind, a time of "singing, dancing, rejoicing, jubilating." Therefore, many who heard of Boehme's remarkable spiritual experience believed that in him the words of Paracelsus had come true. He had, to use his own words, "wrestled in God's presence a considerable time for the knightly crown... which later, with the breaking of the gate in the deep center of nature, I attained with much joy.

Their enthusiasm, however, was not universally shared. A copy of the manuscript of *Aurora* fell by chance into the hands of the Lutheran Pastor Primarius Gregorius Richter of Goerlitz. The clergyman read the pages that John Wesley was later to describe as "sublime nonsense, inimitable bombast, fustian not to be paralleled," and the celebrated English Bishop Warburton characterized as something that "would disgrace Bedlam at full moon." Richter went to his pulpit the next Sunday and poured out his indignation upon Boehme's work. Among the congregation that morning sat Jacob Boehme himself, who listened quietly and without a shadow of emotion to the stern denunciations of his pastor. Afterward, he went to Richter and attempted to explain those passages of *Aurora* to which the latter took most violent exception. But the clergyman would have neither Boehme nor his book, and asked the town council to expel Boehme from Goerlitz. His effort failed, but the justices warned Boehme that since he was a shoemaker, he must abandon writing and stick to the trade for which he was licensed. Boehme, who had said, "In Yes and No all things consist," accepted their injunction, and entered upon still another time of silence. This period lasted from 1612, the year the King James Version of the English Bible was issued, until 1619, when a Dutch ship landed in Jamestown, Virginia, with the first African slaves to be sold in North America.

Meanwhile, Jacob Boehme's fame was spreading as more and more people read the manuscript copies of his *Aurora*, which were circulated by his admirers. Among the latter were the physician of Goerlitz, the learned Dr. Tobias Kober; the director of the elector of Saxony's chemical laboratory at Dresden, Dr. Balthazar Walther; the nobleman Carl Ender van Sercha; and the Paracelsus student, who was to be Boehme's biographer, Abraham von Franckenberg.

Again and again these men urged Boehme to ignore the order of the magistrates of Goerlitz, and to continue his writing, but he consistently refused. However, early in 1619 their urgings met with success, and Boehme resumed his writing, and continued with increasing zeal during the following years. As he wrote, "I had resolved to do nothing in future, but to be quiet before God in obedience, and to let the devil with all his host sweep over me. But with me it was as when a seed is hidden in the earth. Contrary to all reason, it grows up in storm and rough weather. In the winter, all is dead, and reason says, 'Everything is ended for it.' But the precious seed within me sprouted and grew green, oblivious of all storms, and, amid disgrace and ridicule, it has blossomed into a lily!"

Through all the following years Boehme remained faithful to his original conviction that everything he wrote was not the fruit of his own intellectual creativeness, but was the gift of the spiritual world. In 1620, the memorable year of the Pilgrim Fathers at Plymouth, he said, "I did not dare to write other than as I was guided. I have continued writing as the Spirit directed, and have not given place to reason."

Boehme was one of those people who suffer much from the enthusiasm and admiration of their friends. The latter were responsible for the attack by Pastor Primarius Richter, because of their circulating copies of *Aurora*, as we have seen. Again, toward the end of 1623, Boehme's friend, Sigismund von Schweinitz published three small works of Boehme, the first of the latter's writings to appear in print. Immediately the enemy in the person of clergyman Richter attacked Jacob Boehme, and once again complained to the magistrates of Goerlitz. This time, since he had broken their injunction against his writing, they ordered Boehme to leave town.

Before receiving the sentence of the magistrates, Boehme had been invited to visit the court of the elector of Saxony in Dresden. Therefore, early in May, the shoemaker-exile from Goerlitz arrived in Dresden to attend a "conference of noble people," as he described it.

Boehme was fast becoming famous. The second attack upon him by Pastor Primarius Richter was known widely, and the sale of his writings, which were rapidly appearing in print, steadily increased. He was convinced that in only a short time "the nations will take up what my native town is casting away." He regarded the invitation to the elector's court as an opportunity to defend his works before some of the leading theologians and scholars of his time, and he was right.

His devoted student, Dr. Balthasar Walther, had arranged that Boehme was to be a guest in the home of Dr. Benedict Hinckelmann, Walther's successor as director of the elector's laboratory and the court physician. Boehme's reception in Dresden was all that his most devoted friends could have desired. He was entertained with consideration and appreciation, and he found that important members of the court circle had studied his writings and welcomed this opportunity to discuss them with him. One of the prominent noblemen of the elector's household, Joachim van Loss, invited Boehme to visit his castle in order that they might have conversation together. Major Stahlmeister, chief master of horse to the Elector, did everything possible to inform the Elector favorably concerning Boehme's work.

Finally, at the request of the elector, Boehme was examined orally by six eminently learned doctors of theology and by two mathematicians. As a contemporary account describes it, "The illustrious Elector found great satisfaction in Boehme's answers. He asked Boehme to come to him privately, spoke with him, extended many favors to him, and gave him permission to return to his home in Goerlitz."

At the conclusion of his visit, which lasted nearly two months, Boehme left Dresden, his teachings at least partly accepted. He did not return directly to Goerlitz, but visited three of his noblemen friends on the way. At the home of one of them he was taken ill, and as soon as possible, he hastened home to Goerlitz, where his friend and physician, Dr. Tobias Kober undertook his care. It was not long, however, before Dr. Kober, realizing that Jacob Boehme's death was near, arranged that he should receive the sacrament of the Lord's Supper after he had made a confession of faith. This was done on November, 1624.

It was nearly two o'clock in the morning of the following Sunday that Jacob Boehme asked his son, Tobias, "Do you hear that beautiful music, my son?" Tobias replied that he did not. Then Boehme said, "Open the door then, so we can hear it better." He inquired as to the hour, and when he was told that it was not yet three oclock, he replied, "Then my time has not yet come."

With the first faint touches of Aurora on the eastern sky, Jacob Boehme spoke words of farewell to his wife and children, and with a smile of joyful expectancy on his face, breathed out his spirit with the words, "Now I go to Paradise!"

A great crowd of the everyday people of Goerlitz, the shoemakers, tanners, craftsmen, along with devoted students of Boehme's writings, attended his funeral. The pall-bearers were shoemakers of Goerlitz, and the funeral service was conducted by the Lutheran clergyman who succeeded Richter. On the tombstone of porphry are inscribed the words, "Jacob Boehme, *philosophus Teutonicus.*"

Jacob Boehme once described life as a "curious bath of thorns and thistles," and his experience witnessed the truth of his words. But all the difficulties of his comparatively short life of forty-nine years were more than compensated by his vision of the greatness of humankind and of our destiny. As he wrote, "We have a spark of the spirit as a supernatural gift of God, to bring forth by degrees a new birth of that life which was lost in Paradise. This sacred spark of the divine nature within us has a natural, strong, almost infinite longing for that eternal spirit of God from which it came forth. It came forth from God, it came out of God; therefore it is always in a state of return to God. All this is called the breathing, the quickening of the Holy Spirit within us, which are so many operations of this spark of life, tending toward God."

10

In 1548, the year Michelangelo was made chief architect of St. Peter's in Rome, Giordano Bruno was born beneath the shadow of Mount Vesuvius in the little village of Cicala near Nola. His boyhood was passed in the midst of earthquakes, plagues, and famine, while robbers and outlaws frequented the hills and fields of his native countryside. His father was a soldier, and the boy was named Philip.

At the age of fifteen he was enrolled in the Dominican monastery in Naples, the same cloister where Thomas Aquinas had lived three hundred years before. There he was given the name Giordano, which had been the name of one of the intimate companions of St. Dominic himself.

For nearly thirteen years he studied in this monastery, and became learned in the works of the ancient philosophers, particularly of Plotinus and Pythagoras. He was of an independent spirit, and gave considerable concern to his censor on this account. For example, he removed the saints' pictures from his cell, leaving only the crucifix on the wall. When he discovered a monk reading *The Seven Joys of Mary*, he advised him to read something more rational. He also questioned points in the Church dogma such as the Transsubstantiation, the Trinity, and the Immaculate Conception. At an early age he was deeply impressed with the scientific writings of Copernicus, and after some twenty years of reading them recalled that the force of their teaching still worked strongly upon him.

The teachings of the Neo-Platonists and of Nicholas of Cusa formed the basis of his own philosophy, and during his early years he wrote considerable poetry as well.

In 1572, when Bruno was twenty-four, he took holy orders, read his first Mass, and began to perform the other priestly functions. About this time he took some of his companions into his confidence, and frankly told them some of the questions he entertained on matters of Church dogma. They lost no time in informing their superiors, and soon the Holy Office of the Inquisition reprimanded

Bruno sharply. Plans were made to bring him before a court of the Inquisition, but Bruno secretly left Naples and went to Rome, where he stayed in the Della Minerva Monastery.

However, he was not long left in peace. Fra Domenico Vito, provincial of the Order, charged him with heresy, and orders for his arrest were sent to Rome. Letters from friends informed Bruno that soon after his departure from Naples his books, which he had hidden, had been discovered, including works by Chrisostom and Hieronymous with notes by Erasmus. Bruno's situation was very serious, and he left the monastery, divested himself of his Dominican habit, and wandered over the Campagna in the vicinity of the ruins of Hadrian's villa dressed as a poor beggar, which indeed he was. These events occurred in 1576–1577, at about the time of the birth of the painter, Peter Paul Rubens.

Now began Bruno's years of wandering, during which he sought to make known the new teachings about the universe as set forth by Copernicus. He also continued his own writings, creating philosophical masterpieces and poetic works of unusual mystical depth and content. He took passage in a ship bound for Genoa, but was unable to land because of the plague and civil war. Therefore he stopped at Noli, on the Riviera, where he taught boys grammar and delivered lectures on the work of Copernicus, the plurality of worlds, and the shape of the earth. But this was too much for the local clergy, and once again Bruno wandered, this time to Turin, where he hoped to obtain an opportunity to lecture in the university through the celebrated patron of scholars, Duke Emmanuele Filberto. However, the latter was under the influence of the Jesuits, and once again Bruno was denied the post he sought.

Bruno reached Venice after traveling across northern Italy from Turin, but here, too, he found that the deadly plague had done its work as in Genoa, and a large part of the inhabitants—including the painter Titian at the age of ninety-nine—had died. However, Venice was the center of the publishing activities of Italy, and Bruno braved the plague in order to have some of his work printed there. Shortly afterward he visited the Dominicans at Padua, and "they persuaded me to wear the habit again, even though I would not profess the religion it implied, because they said it would help in my travels to be thus dressed. And so I put on the white cloth robe and the hood which I had kept by me when I left Rome."

When Bruno arrived in Geneva, the Marchese Galcazzo Carraciola, nephew of Pope Paul IV, also a refugee from persecution by the church, and a member of the Calvinist Protestant religion, befriended him. The Marchese asked him to cease wearing the Dominican habit and to assume the usual dress of the lay scholar, and Bruno did so, never again wearing a religious habit. During his stay in Geneva, Bruno found himself in trouble with Antoine de la Faye, a member of the Academy, because he took exception to one of the latter's lectures and attacked some twenty points in it. Bruno was arrested and imprisoned for a short time, and after his release was informed that he must either adopt Calvinism or leave the city.

Shortly after this Bruno entered France, visiting Lyons and afterwards Toulouse. In the latter place he received his doctor's degree, and held the position of professor of philosophy in the university for two years, lecturing to appreciative hearers on astronomy and general philosophical subjects. But again the clergy interfered with his work, and he left Toulouse for Paris, where he arrived in 1581.

Henry III, king of France, had heard of Bruno's great gifts as a lecturer, and of his unusual learning, eloquence and memory. Therefore, he wished to appoint Bruno to the faculty of the Sorbonne, but before doing so, it was necessary for Bruno to confess and attend Mass as a professing Catholic. Bruno fearlessly and uncompromisingly refused, and so greatly did his honesty and sincerity impress the king that the latter allowed him to assume the position without regard to his scruples concerning religion.

The Paris lectures of Giordano Bruno were based on his study of the famous treatise, the *Ars Magna*, which Ramon Llull, the eminent Majorcan author, Arabic scholar, mystic, educational reformer, and traveller, had written in 1275. In addition, Bruno discussed logic, general philosophy, astronomy, the symbolism of Pythagoras, and the teachings of Copernicus.

After two years' teaching in Paris, Bruno was offered the post of secretary to Michel de Castelnau, sieur de Mauvissiere, ambassador to England. Bruno found London in a ferment of excitement, since attempts had recently been made on the life of Queen Elizabeth. Added to this were the constant rumors that the Spanish were preparing to launch a massive invasion attempt against the coasts of England. Indeed, after Bruno had been in England for about a year, these rumors were confirmed by accurate information that a great Armada was gathering in the Tagus with designs upon England.

But politics, rumors of invasion, and tales of military exploit did not interest Bruno. He visited Oxford, and was disappointed with what he found there. From the time he first landed in the country, he had been repelled by what he considered the brutality of English manners in contrast with those he had known in Italy and France. In Protestant Oxford, Bruno found a narrowness and sectarian dogmatism entirely foreign to the ideas of objective freedom he believed should prevail among scholars. The presence of the distinguished Polish Prince Johann a Lesco at Oxford was the occasion for a debate in which Bruno defended his new cosmology based on the teachings of the Polish Copernicus, against a group of theologians. Bruno won easily, but was soon forbidden to continue his lectures in Oxford.

While Bruno found the manners of the British distasteful and the attitude of the Oxford scholars hopelessly bigoted, in the person of the Queen he found something to admire. He was frequently invited to private conversations with Elizabeth, who was always happy when she could display her knowledge of Italian, and who appreciated Bruno's learning and charm. In London, Bruno met the brilliant statesman Sir Philip Sydney to whom he dedicated one of his works, Lord Bacon of Verulam, and other prominent figures of the Elizabethan court. Bruno's duties at the embassy apparently were not arduous, since he seems to have had time to mingle with the court, to form acquaintances with the leading men of the time (there is a tradition that he met Shakespeare in the printing shop of Thomas Vautrollier), to hold lectures at Oxford, and—most important for posterity—to devote himself to writing.

In 1584, while Sir Walter Raleigh's expedition in Virginia was taking place, and the plot involving Mary Queen of Scots was fast coming to a head, Bruno wrote his two most famous metaphysical works, *De la Causa, Principio, ed Uno*, and *D l'Infinito, Universo, e Mondi*.

Early in 1585, with the plans for an English invasion of the Netherlands taking shape, and the raids on the Spanish American coasts by Sir Francis Drake making certain a crisis with Spain, the French ambassador decided he should return to France for a time. Therefore, Bruno left England, probably not too unwillingly, though the years of his English residence were among the most productive and happiest of his life.

Bruno's ideas were found acceptable to the superiors of the college of Cambrai, and he found a temporary place among the lecturers there. However, his outspokenness brought him into trouble, for he prepared a thesis of one hundred twenty articles, in which he attacked the philosophy of Aristotle. His works and teaching evoked enthusiasm such as had not been witnessed in academic circles in France since the times of Abelard. Bruno's theses were printed by permission of the censor, and the debate on them was held on May 25, 1588, at Whitsuntide.

At once after his triumph, Bruno left France for Germany, where he hoped to find freedom to lecture. In Marburg he was disappointed, but in Wittenberg he was welcomed, and found the atmosphere congenial to his creative activity. There he produced several more written works.

In 1588, the Spanish Armadawas defeated, and with it the hope of Philip II to crush English Protestantism under the tread of invading Spanish Catholic armies. Bruno decided to visit Prague, and from there he went to the university at Helmstadt where he remained for a year, until he was driven out by the attacks of Boethius, Lutheran Rector of Helmstadt. Bruno decided to go to Frankfort, where he hoped to prepare and publish several works, but he was not allowed to enter the city. Instead, he found refuge in a Carmelite cloister just outside the city through the kind assistance of the famous publishers Wechel and Fischer. In the cloister he worked with feverish haste, and produced a number of works, which were then published. The prior of the monastery recalled Bruno as "a man of universal mind, skillful in all sciences, but without a trace of religion."

During this period—when he wrote his *Seven Liberal Arts*—the Frankfort Fair took place, and many publishers from foreign countries were present. There Bruno met the Venetian booksellers Bertano and Ciotto, and it was the latter who took Bruno's writings to Venice where they were found by a young nobleman, Giovanni Mocenigo, who read them with great interest and inquired for details about the author.

Sometime later, when Bruno was in Zurich, a letter reached him from the young Mocenigo, inviting him to visit him in Venice and promising him safe conduct for the journey. As soon as Bruno's friends heard of the invitation, they urged him not to accept it, for they feared for his safety at the hands of the inquisition. But Bruno brushed their fears aside. He had confidence in this young nobleman, a member of one of the finest and most honorable families of Venice. Therefore, Bruno crossed the Alps and descended into Italy, arriving in Venice in October 1591.

The first months after Bruno's arrival were filled with scholarly activity. He began to tutor the young Mocenigo, and also lectured privately to German students at Padua, where he was soon to be followed by Galileo. Bruno frequented the Venetian philosophical and literary societies, and was welcomed in the home of Andrea Morosini and of his student Mocenigo. Finally, after some time Bruno decided that he would like to return to Frankfort to publish some of his works there. But this was not to be. From the moment he had arrived in Italy the spies of the Inquisition were on his track, and Giovanni Mocenigo cooperated with them. Now that Bruno wished to leave the country, Mocenigo had him arrested and thrown into the prison of the Inquisition. He was charged with many heresies, most serious being his teaching of the infinity of the universe.

Bruno was kept in the prison at Venice for nine months, and at the end of that time was taken in chains to the Bridge of Sighs and then conveyed through the lagoons to Ancona, where he remained until he was taken to Rome. After torture and solitary confinement at Ancona, Bruno was turned over to the Roman Inquisition, and for seven years he experienced the terrors of the prison of the Holy Office. To the last he refused to give up his beliefs and defied his opponents in all they brought against him. On February 9, 1600, Bruno was excommunicated with the cries of "Anathema."

On February 16 in the Campo dei Fiori, a Roman flower market, Giordano Bruno was burned at the stake. He was hardly fifty years of age, and his body showed signs of dreadful torture. With his head erect, his eyes showing full consciousness, he walked unassisted to the stake.

Rudolf Steiner said in a lecture on January 12, 1923, "The flaming pyre in which Giordano Bruno was put to death in the year 1600 was an outer sign of a most significant phase of inner development.... The flames in Rome are a glorious memorial in history, as Giordano Bruno himself indicated. While he was burning, he said, Something *will* come into being. And what was destined to come into being, what drew forth his cry, 'You can put me to death, but not through centuries will my ideas be able to be put to death'—that is precisely what must live on."

11

Shortly after the beginning of the Thirty Years' War, in the year Virginia became a royal colony with governor and council appointed by the British crown, and two years after New Netherlands was established as a Dutch colony in America, Johannes Scheffler was born in the German city of Breslau in Silesia, in 1624, the year Jacob Boehme died. When Johannes was five, his mother enrolled him and his brother at the Elizabeth Gymnasium in Breslau, shortly before her death. At the age of nineteen Johannes Scheffler matriculated at the University of Strassburg, where he intended to study medicine and law. After a year at Strassburg, he entered the University of Leyden and remained there two years. While he was at Leyden Scheffler discovered the works of Jacob Boehme, which had been published at Amsterdam in 1642. As he expressed it, "When one is in Holland, all sorts of things come one's way."

From Leyden, Scheffler went to the greatest medical school at that time, the University of Padua, where he received his degree of Doctor of Medicine and Philosophy in 1648.

At about this time he wrote in the album of one of his fellow students, *Mundus nihil pulcherrimum,* The world is a very beautiful Nothing. In 1649 Johannes Scheffler was appointed court physician to the strict Lutheran Duke Sylvanus Nimrod at Oels in Württemberg. Shortly before Scheffler arrived in Oels, the town of four thousand inhabitants had been reduced to less than two thousand, due to an action which had been fought there in the Thirty Years' War. The cattle had been killed, crops destroyed, houses ruined, and even the castle of the Duke was slightly damaged.

At the same time that Scheffler came to Oels, an older man also arrived in the town. He had been born there fifty-six years before, and was destined to play an important role in the life of Scheffler. This man was Abraham von Franckenberg, whom we have already met as the friend and biographer of Boehme; as Scheffler's friend he was to guide the latter on his spiritual path.

Years before, von Franckenberg had given over his estate to his eldest son, and had reserved only two small rooms in the house for himself, where he studied and lived. During the plagues that swept over the district from time to time, he was of great help to the sick. It was at a time of plague that he met Jacob Boehme, and eventually printed the latter's writings at his own expense. Von Franckenberg studied Kaballa, alchemy, and the works of Giordano Bruno and Copernicus with the single aim of solving the secrets of the science of nature. Because of his studies von Franckenberg was attacked by the Lutheran clergy; he finally left Oels in 1641 and went to Danzig where he lived for eight years as the guest of the famous astronomer, Helvelius. From Danzig he returned to Oels in 1649. When he was asked by the duke if he was a Catholic, a Lutheran, or a Calvinist, von Franckenberg answered, "I am the heart of all these religions."

Johannes Scheffler was attracted to van Franckenberg at their first meeting, and soon the young physician became the devoted student of the older scientist. Long hours were spent by the two of them in von Franckenberg's little rooms discussing Boehme, alchemy, astronomy, the mystics of medieval times, and so on. Two and one-half years after their meeting, von Franckenberg died, and he bequeathed many of his precious books and manuscripts to Scheffler. Among these works, which Scheffler referred to as a "real pharmacy of the soul," were the *Theologia Germanica*, the writings of Boehme, Weigel, Paracelsus, Bruno, Tauler, and Rulman Merswin. One volume of this collection is preserved, bearing the date 1652 inscribed on the flyleaf and, in the handwriting of Scheffler, the words, "From my faithful friend, Abraham van Franckenberg." Another volume from this collection also contains extensive notations in Scheffler's handwriting.

Shortly after van Franckenberg's death, Scheffler decided to write a book composed of passages from his favorite mystical authors. This he intended to issue as a New Year gift volume. As a matter of course, the printer submitted the book to Christoph Freytag, court chaplain and censor. Freytag struck out long passages, and not only refused to give his imprimatur, but also declined to so much as speak with Scheffler about it. This was a turning-point in Scheffler's spiritual life. He realized that the Lutheran church could no longer be his religious home. He resigned his post, left Oels immediately, and returned to Breslau.

Among the writers whom Scheffler had quoted in his book, many were Catholic. Now he began to read Catholic books more and more, spending some months in Breslau in thorough study of them. On June 12, 1653, Johannes Scheffler embraced the Roman Catholic faith.

As Abraham von Franckenberg had been a strong influence in Scheffler's life at one point, now a second man exerted a powerful effect upon him. This was Sebastian von Rostock, born the son of a poor ropemaker, now the vicar general of the diocese of Breslau. As a simple parish priest in the village of Niesse he had witnessed the hardships of the Thirty Years' War. For example, when the Lutheran armies rounded up many Catholics and imprisoned them in buildings, he risked his life by climbing in the windows to give them spiritual consolation. One day while he was walking through the forest, he was set upon by a Lutheran cavalryman. He drew his sword, which all men, clergymen or not, had to wear at that time for self-protection. He returned the attack, and mortally wounded his opponent. However, the instant the cavalryman fell from his horse, von Rostock rushed to him in order to give him absolution that he might die in a state of grace. In the Catholic Counter-Reformation of 1653–1654, van Rostock was extremely severe on the Lutherans, with the result that over two hundred fifty churches were returned to Catholic use in Silesia alone.

At this point, however, von Rostock wished to have some proof that Lutherans were finding it possible to embrace the Catholic faith without pressure or force. Therefore, the free conversion of the celebrated former court physician, Johannes Scheffler, was precisely the example he was looking for. He sought out Scheffler, who by this time had decided to change his name. First Scheffler adopted the name of Johannes de Angelis, a Spanish mystic of the sixteenth century, calling himself Johannes Angelus. But he discovered that there existed a certain Protestant doctor of theology, Johannes Angelus of Darmstadt, so he added "Silesius" from his birthplace, calling himself Johannes Angelus Silesius, by which he is known to posterity.

Sebastian von Rostock invited Angelus Silesius to his palace, and after talking with him arranged that the Austrian Emperor, Frederick III would give him the title of Court physician, but without either duties or salary. Nevertheless, the title alone gave Angelus Silesius good reputation, particularly in Catholic circles. More important, however, is the fact that von Rostock give his imprimatur to Angelus Silesius' *Witty Sayings and End-Rhymes* (*Geistreiche Sinn and Schlussreime*), which, when it was reprinted in 1674 was given the name by which it has since become famous, *The Cherubinic Wanderer*. The book was approved in July, 1656, but was not published until 1657, the year before the birth of the English composer, Henry Purcell. In 1674, Angelus Silesius' collection of some two hundred poems was published under the title *Holy Ecstasies, or Sacred Shepherd Songs in Adoration of Jesus*. From this collection, several poems were eventually included in the Lutheran hymnal, and today they are among the best-loved hymns of the Protestant church.

Angelus Silesius became extremely zealous in developing the activities of the Catholic church in Breslau. Now a Franciscan priest, he organized the first Catholic procession held in Breslau for well over a century. And to drive the lesson home to observers, Angelus Silesius himself carried the cross and wore the crown of thorns in the procession. The next twelve years were a period of intense controversy, for in that time Angelus Silesius wrote and published some fifty-five attacks on Protestantism, most of them extremely bitter. Finally he was persuaded to give up this activity by the superior of his order.

In 1664, Angelus Silesius was appointed marshal and counsellor to Sebastian von Rostock, who meanwhile had become prince-bishop of Breslau. Seven years later, when the prince-bishop died suddenly, a sadness settled upon Angelus Silesius that did not leave him until own death.

Just as Sebastian von Rostock had appeared after the death of Abraham von Franckenberg, now a third man befriended Angelus Silesius. This was Bernard Rose, Abbot of the Cistercian monastery of Grussau and Vicar General of the Cistercians in Silesia. Abbot Rose was a man of great strength, kindness of heart, a stern disciplinarian in his monastery, and a firm supporter of the Counter-Reformation. The monastery of Grussau was located about fifty miles from Breslau and was noted for its hospitality to all who knocked at its gates.

Angelus Silesius was received with much warmth and kindliness at Grussau. He found understanding, support, and comfort, of inestimable value to him, since now he was a dying man. The months he lived at Grussau were spent in writing, meditation, and prayer. There he completed his last work, the *Ecclesiologia,* which he dedicated to Abbot Bernard Rose, his friend. The last three months of Angelus Silesius' life were marked by severe suffering, but through it all he was able to maintain an attitude of inner calm, of lofty spiritual vision, and of clear consciousness. He died on July 9, 1677, and to the last moment of his life he never ceased to manifest the spirit of love and peace that had settled upon him during his severe illness. In his last days Angelus Silesius repeated again and again, "Tranquillity is the best treasure that one can have."

* * *

In the Loggia di San Paolo on the south side of the square, opposite the Church of Santa Maria Novella in Florence, is a famous terra cotta relief created by Andrea della Robbia sometime around 1492. Influenced by a work of Fra Angelico, it depicts the historic meeting between St. Francis and St. Dominic. When one contemplates what is represented there, one is reminded of the Scripture, "Mercy and truth are met together." An Italian, whose life-work was centered in a love that is ever merciful, embraces a Spaniard, whose striving for truth was expressed in knowledge of the eternal spirit.

Rudolf Steiner once observed that "External events, which at first glance seem to be trifling occurrences in the course of history, are deeply and inwardly rooted in the evolution of mankind."

In this sense, this artistic creation—fashioned at the moment of emergence of the modern world, portraying the meeting of the founders of two great streams of spiritual aspiration that arose in the Middle Ages, and bearing the classic Platonic and Aristotelian impulses into later times—expresses their significance in the development of humankind.

The series of eleven men, around whom this book is created, begins with Meister Eckhart, a Dominican, and concludes with

Angelus Silesius, a Franciscan. Midway between the two Rudolf Steiner places Henry Cornelius, Agrippa of Nettesheim, typical of the "new human" of the Renaissance: scholar, courtier, diplomat, physician, and master of the "new learning" that came to the fore at the dawn of the modern age. Between the Dominicans, for whom the ideal picture of the world was embodied in the word *order*, and the Franciscans, for whom the essence of creation was expressed in the word *love*, Rudolf Steiner has placed the figure whom he calls "a protagonist for a genuine science of nature."

In the lives of these eleven men is united the progressive unfolding of ideas and events at a moment of supreme importance in the course of human life on earth. The struggles, tensions, and resolutions epitomize the historical process as it unveiled itself in the important development then taking place in the evolution of humanity. In their life-experiences we see the birth-pangs of the appearance of a new stage in the life of humankind—the dawn of the modern age.

Preface to the First Edition
1901

This work discusses the content of my lectures given at the theosophical library in Berlin last winter. Count and Countess Brockdorff invited me to speak on mysticism to an audience who considered such matters vitally important. Ten years ago, I would not have dared agree to such a request. This does not imply that the world of ideas I express today was not alive in me then. This world of ideas is, in fact, fully contained in my *Intuitive Thinking as a Spiritual Path: A Philosophy of Freedom,* written in 1894. But to express this realm of ideas as I do today and to make it the basis of a discussion, as I did in this work, requires something more than an unshakable conviction of its conceptual truth. It requires an intimate familiarity with these ideas, which is gained only with many years of living. Finally, now that I have gained this familiarity, I dare to speak as you will find I have in this work.

Those who do not meet my ideas with an *open mind* will discover contradiction upon contradiction here. I recently dedicated a book on nineteenth-century philosophy (Berlin, 1900) to the great scientist Ernst Haeckel; a book I ended by justifying his ideas. In the expositions in this book, I speak with assenting devotion concerning certain mystics, from Meister Eckhart to Angelus Silesius. People might mention other "contradictions" that I ignore altogether here. I am not surprised when one faction accuses me of being a "mystic" and another of being a "materialist." If I find that the Jesuit priest Müller has solved a difficult chemical problem, and if I happen agree with him without qualification in this *particular* matter, only a fool could accuse me of being an adherent of Jesuitism.

Those who go their own way, as I do, will certainly be subjected to many misunderstandings. Fundamentally, however, they can easily deal with it. Such misunderstandings are usually obvious once the mentality of those critics is considered. It is not without humor that I recall the many "critical" judgments leveled at me during my career as a writer. In the beginning it all went well; I wrote about Goethe and related subjects. Many people felt that they could fit what I had to say into their preconceived notions by saying, "We can honestly characterize works such as Steiner's introductions to Goethe's scientific writings as the best writings on this matter."

By the time I published an independent work later on, I had become much more stupid. Now a benevolent critic offered this advice: "Before he continues to revise and publish his *Intuitive Thinking as a Spiritual Path*, one must urgently advise that he first come to an understanding of those two philosophers [Hume and Kant]." Unfortunately, that critic knows only what he manages to read in Kant and Hume; he is really advising me to see only what he sees in those thinkers. Once I have accomplished that, he will find me satisfactory. When *Intuitive Thinking as a Spiritual Path* was published, I was judged as though I were the most empty-headed novice. I happened to receive this judgment from a gentleman who feels compelled to write books because of the innumerable volumes by others—which he has failed to understand. He thoughtfully informs me that I would have noticed my mistakes if I "had pursued my studies of psychology, logic, and epistemology more deeply." And he immediately lists for me all the books I should read to become as smart as he—Mill, Sigwart, Wundt, Riehl, Paulsen, B. Erdmane.

Especially diverting for me was the advice of a man who is so impressed with his own "understanding" of Kant that he cannot imagine anyone can really *read* Kant and not share his opinion. Consequently, he point out to me the relevant chapters in Kant's writings that might help me to understand Kant as profoundly as he does.

I present here a few *typical* judgments of my ideas. Although in themselves they are insignificant, they nevertheless appear to me well-suited to point out, in a symptomatic sense, certain facts that now constitute serious obstacles in the path of those who write on matters of higher knowledge. I must follow my own path regardless of the good advice I am given about reading Kant or accusations of heresy because I agree with Haeckel. Therefore, I have written about mysticism without being concerned about the judgments of a credulous materialist. To avoid wasting any printer's ink, I would like simply to inform those who might advise me now to read Haeckel's *The Riddle of the Universe* that in the last months I have presented about thirty lectures on the book.

I hope I have shown in my work that one can faithfully follow scientific philosophy and still seek out the paths *to the soul*, into which mysticism leads, *when properly understood*. I go even further and assert that only those who understand spirit in the sense of *true* mysticism can fully understand the reality of nature. But people must beware of confusing true mysticism with the "mysticism" of muddled heads. I have shown how mysticism can err in *Intuitive Thinking as a Spiritual Path: A Philosophy of Freedom*.

Rudolf Steiner
BERLIN
September, 1901

Bibliography & Further Reading

Works by Rudolf Steiner

Anthroposophical Leading Thoughts. London: Rudolf Steiner Press, 1998.

Anthroposophy (A Fragment): A New Foundation for the Study of Human Nature. Hudson, NY: Anthroposophic Press, 1996.

Anthroposophy and the Inner Life. Bristol, UK: Rudolf Steiner Press, 1994.

Autobiography: Chapters in the Course of My Life, 1861–1907. Hudson, NY: Anthroposophic Press, 1999.

The Boundaries of Natural Science. Hudson, NY: Anthroposophic Press, 1983.

Christianity as Mystical Fact. Hudson, NY: Anthroposophic Press, 1997.

The Christian Mystery. Hudson, NY: Anthroposophic Press, 1998.

Cosmic Memory. Blauvelt, NY: Garber Communications, 1990.

The Effects of Esoteric Development. Hudson, NY: Anthroposophic Press, 1997.

The Evolution of Consciousness as Revealed through Initiation-Knowledge. Sussex, UK: Rudolf Steiner Press, 1991.

The Foundations of Human Experience. Hudson, NY: Anthroposophic Press, 1996 (previously *Study of Man*).

Founding a Science of the Spirit. London: Rudolf Steiner Press, 1999 (previously *At the Gates of Spiritual Science*).

The Gospel of St. John. Hudson, NY: Anthroposophic Press, 1984.

The Gospel of St. Luke. London: Rudolf Steiner Press, 1988.

The Gospel of St. Mark. Hudson, NY: Anthroposophic Press, 1986.

The Gospel of St. Matthew. London: Rudolf Steiner Press, 1986.

Guidance in Esoteric Training: From the Esoteric School. London: Rudolf Steiner Press, 1998.

How to Know Higher Worlds. Hudson, NY: Anthroposophic Press, 1994.

Individualism in Philosophy. Spring Valley, NY: Mercury Press, 1989.

The Riddles of Philosophy. Hudson, NY: Anthroposophic Press, 1973.

Riddles of the Soul. Spring Valley, NY: Mercury Press, 1996.

Spiritual Beings in the Heavenly Bodies and in the Kingdoms of Nature. Hudson, NY: Anthroposophic Press, 1992.

The Spiritual Guidance of the Individual and Humanity. Hudson, NY: Anthroposophic Press, 1992.

The Spiritual Hierarchies and the Physical World: Reality and Illusion. Hudson, NY: Anthroposophic Press, 1996.

A Theory of Knowledge Implicit in Goethe's World Conception. Hudson, NY: Anthroposophic Press, 1988.

Theosophy: An Introduction to the Spiritual Processes in Human Life and in the Cosmos. Hudson, NY: Anthroposophic Press, 1994.

Truth and Knowledge. Blauvelt, NY: Rudolf Steiner Publications, 1981 (also *Truth and Science*. Spring Valley, NY: Mercury Press, 1993).

A Way of Self-Knowledge. Hudson, NY: Anthroposophic Press, 1999.

Works by Other Authors

Agrippa of Nettesheim, Henry Cornelius, *Three Books of Occult Philosophy: The Foundation Book of Western Occultism*. J. Freake, trans., D. Tyson, ed., St. Paul: Llewellyn Publications, 1993.

Barnes, Henry, *A Life for the Spirit: Rudolf Steiner in the Crosscurrents of Our Time*. Hudson, NY: Anthroposophic Press, 1997.

Boehme, Jacob, *Dialogues on the Supersensual Life*. W. Law, ed., New York: Ungar, 1957.

———, *The Aurora*. London: John M. Watkins, 1960.

———, *Epistle*. C. Barker, trans., London: Watkins, 1910.

———, *Dialogues on the Supersensual Life*. New York: Ungar, n.d.

———, *Mysterium Magnum: An Exposition of the First Book of Moses Called Genesis*. J. Sparrow, trans., London: John M. Watkins, 1965.

———, *Sämtliche Schriften*. 8 vols., Will-Erich Peuckert, August Faust, eds., Stuttgart: Frommann, 1955–1961.

———, *The Signature of All Things & Other Discourses*. New York: E. P. Dutton, 1934.

———, *Six Theosophic Points*. Ann Arbor, MI: University of Michigan Press, 1958.

———, *The Three Principles of the Divine Essence*. Spring Valley, NY: St. George Book Service, n.d.

———, *The Way to Christ*. P. Erb, tr., New York: Paulist Press, 1978.

Bruno, Giordano, *The Ash Wednesday Supper (La Cena de la ceneri)*. E. A. Gosselin & L. S. Lerner, eds., Hamden, CN: The Shoe String Press, 1977.

———, *Cause, Principle and Unity (De la Causa, Principio e Uno)*. J. Lindsay, trans., New York: International Publishers, 1962.

———, *On the Composition of Images, Signs & Ideas.* C. Doria, trans, D. Higgins, ed., New York: Willis, Locker & Owens, 1991.

Bynum, Carolyn Walker, *Jesus as Mother: Studies in the Spirituality of the High Middle Ages.* Berkeley/Los Angeles: University of California Press, 1982.

Davies, Oliver, *Meister Eckhart, Mystic Theologian.* London: SPCK, 1991.

Dronke, Peter, *Women Writers of the Middle Ages: A Critical Study of texts from Perpetua (d.203) to Marguerite of Porete (d. 1310).* Cambridge: Cambridge University Press, 1984.

Eckhart, Meister, *The Essential Sermons, Commentaries, Treatises, and Defense.* B. McGinn, trs., New York: Paulist Press, 1981.

———, *Deutsche Werke.* J. Quint, ed., München: Hanser, 1958–1976.

———, *Meister Eckhart: Teacher & Preacher.* B. McGinn, ed., New York: Paulist Press, 1986.

Hollywood, Amy, *The Soul as Virgin Wife: Mechtild of Magdeburg, Marguerite of Porete, and Meister Eckhart.* Notre Dame: University of Notre Dame Press, 1995.

Hopkins, Jasper, *A Miscellany on Nicholas of Cusa.* Minneapolis: The Arthur J. Banning Press, 1994.

Kühlewind, Georg, *From Normal to Healthy: Paths to the Liberation of Consciousness.* Hudson, NY: Lindisfarne Books, 1988.

Llull, Ramon, *L'arbre de philosophie d'amour.* L. Sala-Molins, tr., Paris: Aubier, 1967.

McDermott, Robert (ed.), *The Essential Steiner.* San Francisco: HarperSanFrancisco, 1984.

McGinn, Bernard, *The Flowering of Mysticism: Men and Women in the new Mysticism, 1200–1350.* New York: Crossroad/Herder, 1998.

———, ed. *Meister Eckhart and the Beguine Mystics: Hadewijch of Brabant, Mechtild of Magdeburg and Marguerite of Porete.* New York: Continuum, 1994.

Marchant, Carolyn, *The Death of Nature: Women, Ecology, and the Scientific Revolution.* New York: Harpercollins, 1990.

Mendoza, Ramon G. *The Acentric Labyrinth: Giordano Bruno's Prelude to Contemporary Cosmology.* Rockport, Massachusetts: Element Books, 1995.

Newman, Barbara, *Sister of Wisdom: Saint Hildegard's Theology of the Feminine.* Berkeley: University of California Press, 1987.

Ordine, Nuccio, *Giordano Bruno and the Philosophy of the Ass.* H. Baranski, New Haven, CN: Yale University Press, 1987.

Pagel, Walter. *Joan Baptista Van Helmont: Reformer of Science and Medicine.* Cambridge: Cambridge University Press, 1995.

Paracelsus, *The Hermetic and Alchemical Writings of Paracelsus*, 2 vols. (*Hermetic Chemistry* & *Hermetic Medicine and Hermetic Philosophy*), A. E. Waite, ed., Berkeley: Shambhala, 1976.

Ruusbroec, John, *The Spiritual Espousals and Other Writings,* J. A. Wiseman, trans., New York: Paulist Press, 1985.

Silesius, Angelus, *The Cherubinic Wanderer* (*Classics of Western Spirituality*), New York: Paulist Press, 1986.

Spinoza, Benedict, de, *A Spinoza Reader: The Ethics and Other Works*, New York: Princeton University Press, 1994.

Suso, Henry, *The Exemplar (with Two German Sermons)*, F. Tobin, ed., New York: Paulist Press, 1989.

Tauler, Johannes, *Predigten,* G. Hoffmann, ed., Einseideln: Johannes, 1979.

———, *Sermons,* M. Schrader, tr., New York: Paulist Press, 1985.

Toulmin, Stephen. *Cosmopolis: The Hidden Agenda of Modernity.* Chicago: University of Chicago press, 1992.

Weigel, Valentin, *Sämtliche Schriften*, Will-Erich Peuckert and Winfried Zeller, eds., Stuttgart: Frommann Verlag, 1964.

Yates, Frances A. *Giordano Bruno and the Hermetic Tradition.* Chicago: University of Chicago, 1964.

———, *The Occult Philosophy of the Elizabethan Age*, London: Routledge, 2000.

———, *The Rosicrucian Enlightenment*, London: Routledge, 1993.

Index

A
About the Author, the People, and the Background of this Book 131
Acts of the Apostles 79
Adam 101, 102, 109
Adikes, Erich (1866–1928) 86
Agrippa of Nettesheim (1487–1535) 89
alchemy 103
An Outline of Esoteric Science (Steiner) 88
Anthropology (Topinard) 117
Apollo, oracle of 17
Aquinas, Thomas (1225–1274) 37, 39, 39, 73, 116
Arab 96
Archaeus, or Spiritus vitae 99
Asmus, Paul (1842–1876) 27, 29, 61
astral body 98
Augustine, St. (354–430) 38

B
Bhagavad Gita 30
Boehme, Jacob (1575–1624) 109, 127, 129
Bonaventura, St. (Johannes Fidanza, 1221–1274) 68
Brahe, Tycho (1546–1601) 71
Brentano, Franz (1838–1917) 120
Brockdorff, Count Cay Lorenz von (1844–1921) 197
Brockdorff, Countess Sophie von (1848–1906) 197
Bruno, Giordano (b. Filippo, 1548–1600) 116, 119

C
Cabala 99
Cherubinic Wanderer (Silesius) 33, 121, 126, 129
Constance, Council of 68
Copernicus, Nicolas (1473–1543) 71, 115
Creed, the 128

D
Darwin, Charles (1809–1882) 86, 126, 128
despair 88
Dionysius the Areopagite (c.500) 79
divine spark 69
Du Bois-Reymond, Emil (1818–1896) 25

E
Eckhart, Meister (1260–1328) 19, 37, 49, 51, 65, 67, 72, 77, 79, 99, 105, 197
Egyptians 99
elemental body 98
Eriugena, John Scotus (c.810–c.877) 77, 79
Ethics (Spinoza) 31
evil 110, 112

F
faith 72, 72, 76, 88
Fichte, Johann Gottlieb (1762–1814) 19, 21, 23, 126
four elements 100, 104
Franck, Sebastian (1499–1542) 105

G

Galen, Claudius (129–c.199) 95
Goethe, Johann W. van (1749–1832) 32, 97, 101, 126, 198
grace, light of 74, 108
gravity 72
Greek 96
Greek philosophy 18

H

Haeckel, Ernst Heinrich (1834–1919) 86, 114, 118, 126, 128, 129, 197, 199
Hamerling, Robert (1830–1889) 33
Heavenly Father, the 39, 53
Hegel, Georg Wilhelm Friedrich (1770–1831) 17, 27, 126
Heidel, Wolfgang Ernst (n.d.) 93
Helmholtz, Hermann (1821–1894) 83
History of German Mysticism (Preger) 53
History of Idealism (Willmann) 75
How to Know Higher Worlds (Steiner) 88
Hume, David (1711–1776) 198

I

Ibn Sina (Avicenna) (980–1037) 95, 96
Indo-European Religions (Asmus) 29
intellectual (rational) soul 99
Intuitive Thinking As a Spiritual Path (Steiner) 28, 84, 107, 128, 197, 198, 199
Israelite 96

J

Jesus 105

K

Kant contra Haeckel (Adikes) 86
Kant, Immanuel (1724–1804) 19, 86, 107, 198
Know thyself 17, 18

L

Lamarck, Jean Baptiste (1744–1829) 126
language 20, 22
Linnaeus, Carolus (Carl von Linné, 1707–1778) 102
Llull, Ramon (1235–1315) 119
Luther, Martin (1483–1546) 60

M

Müller (Jesuit priest) 197

N

Neo-Platonism 18, 99
Nicholas of Cusa (1401–1464) 71, 89, 115

P

Paracelsus, Philippus Aureolus Theophrastus (Bombast von Hohenheim, c.1493–1541) 89, 93, 95, 105, 113
Paul, St. 40, 79
Pfeiffer, Franz (1815–1868) 60
Plotinus (205–270) 18
Proclus (410–485) 18

R

Richard of St. Victor (d.1173) 68
Riddle of the Universe (Haeckel) 199
Riddles of Philosophy (Steiner) 84
Riddles of the Soul (Steiner) 88
Ruysbroeck, Jan van (1293–1381) 49, 65, 65, 67

S

Scholasticism 72, 87
Schwenckfeldt, Caspar (1489–1561) 105
Shakespeare (1564–1616) 92
Silesius, Angelus (1624–1677) 19, 32, 120, 121, 126, 127, 129, 197
Solitude, On (Eckhart) 39, 40, 43
Spirit in nature 90
spiritual rebirth 22
spiritual soul 99
spiritualism 67, 91
Stäglin, Elsbet (d.1350) 66
Suso, Heinrich (1295–1366) 49, 65, 66, 67, 77, 105

T

Tauler, Johannes (1300–1361) 21, 49, 72, 77, 81, 105, 120, 127
Theology of Antiquity (Kleutgen) 76
Theory of Knowledge in Goethe's Conception of the World (Steiner) 70, 129
Topinard, Paul (1830–1911) 117
Trithemius, Abbot Johannes (1462–1516) 90, 93

V

Verses in Prose (Goethe) 32

W

Weigel, Valentin (1533–1588) 18, 105
Werner, Karl (1821–1888) 74
Willmann, Otto (1839–1920) 75

Y

Yliaster 100

Z

Zschopau 18, 105

During the last two decades of the nineteenth century, the Austrian-born Rudolf Steiner (1861–1925) became a respected and well-published scientific, literary, and philosophical scholar, particularly known for his work on Goethe's scientific writings. After the turn of the century he began to develop his earlier philosophical principles into an approach to methodical research of psychological and spiritual phenomena. His multifaceted genius has led to innovative and holistic approaches in medicine, philosophy, religion, education (Waldorf schools), special education, economics, science, agriculture (Biodynamic method), architecture, drama, the new arts of speech and eurythmy, and other fields of activity. In 1924 he founded the General Anthroposophical Society, which today has branches throughout the world.

www.ingramcontent.com/pod-product-compliance
Lightning Source LLC
Chambersburg PA
CBHW032253150426
43195CB00008BA/431